Small Teaching

Small Teaching

Everyday Lessons from the Science of Learning

James M. Lang

Second Edition

JB JOSSEY-BASS™
A Wiley Brand

Jossey-Bass
A Wiley Imprint
111 River St, Hoboken, NJ 07030
www.josseybass.com

Library of Congress Cataloging-in-Publication Data

Names: Lang, James M., author.
Title: Small teaching : everyday lessons from the science of learning /
    James M. Lang.
Description: Second edition. | [San Francisco] : Jossey-Bass, [2021] |
    Includes bibliographical references and index.
Identifiers: LCCN 2021024090 (print) | LCCN 2021024091 (ebook) | ISBN
    9781119755548 (cloth) | ISBN 9781119755562 (adobe pdf) | ISBN
    9781119755555 (epub)
Subjects: LCSH: Cognitive learning. | Thought and thinking—Study and
    teaching.
Classification: LCC LB1062 .L349 2021 (print) | LCC LB1062 (ebook) | DDC
    370.15/23—dc23
LC record available at https://lccn.loc.gov/2021024090
LC ebook record available at https://lccn.loc.gov/2021024091

Cover design: Wiley

SECOND EDITION

SKY10028241_072021

For Katie, Madeleine, Jillian, Lucie, and Jack,
who taught me much when they were small

Contents

Acknowledgments

First and foremost, I must express my gratitude for monthly writer's group meetings with Mike Land and Sarah Cavanagh, during which I received wise and helpful feedback on every chapter of this book, both the first and second editions. Mike and Sarah served perfectly as advanced and interested readers, and they made this a better book in every way possible. Special thanks to Sarah for helping me avoid glaring errors in my use of terminology and theories from her home discipline of psychology, and for pointing me to numerous articles that helped thicken my research.

I had the opportunity to present the research from this book—and to test out its applicability to instructors—at many colleges and universities while I was drafting and revising the first edition. So thanks to my hosts and workshop participants at Olds College (Canada), Misericordia University, Regis College, the University of Denver, Fisher College, Florida Institute of Technology, King's Academy (Jordan), MacEwan University (Canada), Indiana State University, the DeLange Conference at Rice University, the University of Texas–San Antonio Health Sciences College, Bucknell University, Georgia Tech, and Columbus State Community College. Thanks as well to the many dozens of institutions around the globe that invited me to share the ideas of this edition with their faculty after the first edition was published. They provided me with a welcome platform to receive feedback upon, and continue to refine the book's theories and models for this second edition.

The seeds for this book were first planted at a meeting with David Brightman at the Teaching Professor Conference in New Orleans, and he was an excellent guide as I worked my way through the conception and proposal stages. His commitment to higher education and to publishing excellent books made him an ideal editor. Pete Gaughan and Connor O'Brien at Wiley proved equally dedicated to the project, and my thanks especially to Connor for his developmental notes on the first draft of the book. The second edition was suggested and shepherded to life by Amy Fandrei, to whom I am grateful as well.

Many colleagues at Assumption University, both faculty and administrative, have been supportive of my work. I am grateful to the University for the two sabbaticals which enabled me first to complete the book and then, six years later, undertake the second edition.

I wrote the vast majority of the first edition at Nu Kitchen in Worcester, Massachusetts. I thank them for all the green tea, about which you will read further in Chapter Two. It seemed to help. The second edition was completed largely at home, as a result of the pandemic. Thanks to DAVIDsTEA for supplying my habit from afar.

I come from a family of teachers; it must have been something in the water where we grew up. I continue to find inspiration from them, especially from my sister, Peggy, who has served as both teacher and principal to urban student populations in Chicago. Also from my brother, Tony, at whose heels I have been tagging along as a student and teacher and writer and human being since we were childhood bunkmates. My mother was the first teacher in the family, and my father continues to teach me to this day.

Much of my extracurricular thinking about learning happens as a result of observing the experiences of my children, to whom this book is dedicated, so thanks to them for the enthusiasm they have always shown for learning, both in and out of school.

Even more of my thinking about education happens as a result of conversations with my wife, an elementary school teacher. For part of the time that I was writing the first edition, I spent Friday mornings volunteering in her kindergarten classroom, and while I was working on the second edition during the pandemic I could hear her teaching her remote kindergarten classes from the dining room all day long. Observing and hearing her teach reminded me constantly of the incredible value of teaching as a profession and of the selfless commitment that so many teachers make to their students. Those reminders continually renewed my inspiration to write this book.

So a final and most heartfelt thanks to Anne—for everything.

About the Author

James M. Lang is a professor of English and director of the D'Amour Center for Teaching Excellence at Assumption University in Worcester, MA. His books about teaching and learning include *Distracted: Why Students Can't Focus and What You Can Do About It* (Basic Books, 2020); *Small Teaching Online: Applying Learning Science in Online Classes* (with Flower Darby, Jossey-Bass, 2019); and *Cheating Lessons: Learning From Academic Dishonesty* (Harvard University Press, 2013). He writes a monthly column on teaching and learning for the *Chronicle of Higher Education*; his work has been appearing in the *Chronicle* since 1999. He edits a series of books on teaching and learning in higher education for West Virginia University Press; he co-edited the second book in the series, *Teaching the Literature Survey Course: New Strategies for College Faculty* (2018). He has conducted workshops on teaching for faculty at more than a hundred colleges or universities in the US and abroad, and consulted for the United Nations on the development of teaching materials in ethics and integrity for college faculty. In September of 2016 he received a Fulbright Specialist grant to work with three universities in Colombia on the creation of a MOOC (massive, open online course) on teaching and learning in STEM education. He has a BA in English and philosophy from the University of Notre Dame, an MA in English from St. Louis University, and a PhD in English from Northwestern University. Follow him on Twitter at @LangOnCourse, on Instagram at @jimlang7 or visit his website at http://www.jamesmlang.com

Preface to the Second Edition

Every year in late December people around the world make resolutions to change their lives. January 1st marks the beginning of new habits and attitudes, new ways of being a good human, and new approaches to the problems and addictions that plague us. I'm one of those people; I especially love to make *big* resolutions. I like it so much I don't limit myself to making them for the new year. My wife has now learned, after many years of living with me, to dread those moments in which I accost her while she's quietly reading her book and pronounce exuberantly: "I've got an incredible idea—it's going to change our lives!" She rolls her eyes, listens to my proposal, nods and smiles, and goes back to her book. She knows to do this because the follow-through on the big resolutions I make typically lasts only until a new one comes along, at which point I track down my wife and let her know that no, that last one was stupid, but *this time* I really have a great idea.

Based on the spate of articles that are published every December and January about New Year's resolutions, I'm not the only one that likes to make resolutions that overshoot my attention or stamina. Those articles almost all make the same point: if you want to make resolutions that stick, start small. You might have a big end goal in mind, but if you want to achieve it, you have to launch your efforts with practical and manageable strategies. In early January of 2021, one of those articles pointed me to the work of BJ Fogg, the director of the Behavior Design Lab at Stanford University. In his book *Tiny Habits: The Small Changes that Change Everything* (2020), Fogg argues that we are most likely to affect real change in our lives when we start with the smallest possible increments we can imagine—if we want to begin developing our upper body strength, for example, we might begin with the plan of doing just two push-ups per day while we are waiting for our coffee to brew. Because that seems like such a small and manageable thing to do, we start the habit, and the habit can then expand until we reach our larger objectives. Our new habits are most likely to stick, Fogg argues, if we can pin them to existing behaviors or moments in our routines (i.e., I always do the push-ups while my tea is steeping) and celebrate our achievements each time we complete the desired behavior (even by just pausing for a moment to congratulate ourselves on another day of doing our push-ups). After I read Fogg's book I was so inspired that I immediately found my wife and pronounced that I had just read something really interesting, and had a great idea about how we could keep our New Year's resolutions and change our lives in the new year. She pointed out that she hadn't made any New Year's resolutions, gave me a nod and a smile, and went back to her book.

Although my non-tiny life resolutions typically don't gain much purchase in my life in the long term, every few years I manage to accomplish one very large task: turning an idea into a book. I don't have a perfect track record on that score either, of course. I make plenty of resolutions to start books that I never finish. But once in a while a big idea emerges that inspires me enough to sit down and start chipping away. In January of 2014, with my failed New Year's resolutions probably fresh in my mind, I wrote the following words in my journal:

> Had a good idea for a book project today for Jossey-Bass: the Five-Minute Intervention, or Teaching on the Edges . . . it's about making brief interventions in a traditional class in order to maximize learning. So faculty don't have to start from scratch in re-thinking their

teaching. Grounded in good cognitive theory, they can make 5–15 minute interventions that allow students to engage with the course and increase their learning potential.

That brief entry was the seed that blossomed into *Small Teaching: Everyday Lessons from the Science of Learning*, first published in the spring of 2016 and now appearing in this second edition. I'm not sure any other book of mine has hewn so closely to its original conception from start to finish. The words above describe with perfect accuracy the book that eventually emerged, and still capture exactly what I hope this book can do for its readers: use research from the learning sciences to offer faculty small, practical changes they can make to their courses in order to improve their students' learning.

The warm reception that this idea received has been one of the greatest surprises of my life. The book has sold more copies than all of my other books combined and seems to find new audiences every semester. I've received hundreds of invitations to give lectures or workshops on the book's ideas to faculty on college and university campuses around the globe. I wrote a multi-part series for the *Chronicle of Higher Education* on small teaching approaches, and those columns have been the most widely-read articles I have ever written. One of those columns in particular, which focused on how to teach effectively in the first five minutes of class, has proven especially popular. I still see it regularly make the rounds on social media, as someone new discovers the unlocked potential of those crucial opening minutes of the class period. In the fall of 2019 we published a sequel, *Small Teaching Online* largely the work of faculty development expert Flower Darby, whose many years of researching and practicing online teaching enabled her to apply the small teaching approach to online courses. As this second edition was heading into production, we were finalizing plans for the third iteration in the series, *Small Teaching* for elementary and middle-school educators.

The small teaching approach was always designed to have two very different appeals to instructors and institutions. First, I wanted to offer pathways to the improvement of teaching and learning that were manageable for faculty, most of whom already have more work than they can handle in their professional and personal lives: teaching multiple classes, serving on committees, doing research in their disciplines, commuting to multiple campuses as adjuncts, raising children, caring for parents, advocating for social justice, surviving a pandemic, and more. As much as they might want to take deep dives into the literature on teaching and learning, they just don't have the time or energy to do so. I tried to make sure all of the techniques in the book were ones that faculty could put into practice without an excessive amount of new preparation or evaluation time. My hope was that faculty members who read *Small Teaching* or attended one of my workshops three days before the semester starts would still be able to squeeze one or two new teaching strategies into their courses that very semester. But even further, I hoped that faculty members who encountered the ideas from the book in the fifth or even tenth week of the semester could still find something new to try with their students before the course ended.

Second, I hoped that these easy-to-apply teaching strategies could have a powerful positive impact on student learning, performance, and retention. Over the course of my own teaching career I have seen how small changes I have made to my own courses could be transformative—could, for example, revitalize a course that had grown stale or change entirely the extent to which students were engaged with the course material. The connection notebooks that you will read about in Chapter Four are the best recent example of that in my own teaching. Using those notebooks, which take very little class time to complete and which require minimal grading from me, has transformed the literature survey courses I teach every year. Through the vehicle of those notebooks, students are able to create much deeper and more meaningful connections between their lives and 19th-century British poems they read for the course. They cite those connection notebooks frequently on our course evaluation forms as one of the aspects of the course that was most helpful to their learning.

To ensure that the small teaching strategies I recommended could have such a positive impact, they had to align with a principle or theory I had encountered in the research on teaching and learning in higher education. Those principles became the foundations for the chapters, enabling me to recommend small teaching changes in a systematic way. One of the major reasons that I wanted to produce a second edition of the book has been that my thinking about those principles has shifted over the last five years. This helps explain the most substantive change you will find in the book: the complete overhaul and re-framing of two chapters, one from Part Two and one from Part Three.

The first edition of the book contained a chapter on "Self-Explaining," which presents research supporting the idea that asking students to talk or write about their learning while they are completing a learning task can deepen their understanding. During the workshops and lectures I gave on the different principles of the book over the last five years, I noticed that this chapter resonated especially with faculty who teach students in more individualized, skill-based settings, such as performing arts or clinical practice in medicine. Faculty outside of those settings had more trouble considering how to incorporate self-explanation in their classrooms. As I reflected on the act of self-explanation, and what made it useful, it occurred to me that *self-explanation* could be considered as one strain of the more general act of *explanation*, and that in fact two of the models in the chapter moved out of the realm of self-explanation and into this more general territory.

Thus, the chapter formerly known as "Self-Explaining" has now been expanded into "Explaining," and presents models for asking students to explain their learning aloud, either to themselves or to their peers or even to audiences outside of the classroom. The three chapters of Part Two now offer a very logical progression of teaching strategies. Learning deepens when students connect course content to their lives outside of the classroom, practice applying their new knowledge and skills in different contexts, and then explain their understanding to someone else. This last activity, of course, is another way of describing what we do as teachers, and we all know how much the practice of teaching enhances our own learning. The same holds true for our students.

Part Three of the first edition contained a chapter on "Growing," which drew from Carol Dweck's research on the growth mindset. Dweck and many others have found that when students believe in the capacity of their intelligence to grow and expand, as opposed to seeing it as fixed and limited, it enhances their ability to learn. The theory of the growth mindset, and its application to education at every level, has been widely promoted and discussed outside of the academy, perhaps more so than any other strategy discussed in the book. The thoroughness of its penetration into educational discourse has prompted the inevitable backlash from those who caution us that instilling a growth mindset into students is no panacea. A fixed mindset is only one of the many barriers that students might face in their efforts to succeed in school, including social and economic ones that require deeper efforts at political change and economic reform. Having acknowledged that, I still see much value in Dweck's theory and its application to education and believe that teachers should know about it.

At the same time, a few years of reflection have helped me realize that what I really wanted to convey in that chapter were techniques that would help students feel like they *belonged* in their classrooms. They belonged there as learners, no matter what their prior educational experiences had been, and they belonged there as valued members of our community, no matter what barriers stood in their way outside of the classroom. Understood through that lens, the growth mindset still fits into that chapter, since a student with a fixed mindset might fear that their limited intellectual capacity means they don't belong in their college or even high school classrooms. But Chapter Seven, re-christened from "Growing" to "Belonging," now includes other strategies to promote belonging, all of them built upon the theoretical foundation of an asset-based approach to teaching. Too often we view our students through a deficit lens, seeing what they lack and trying to fill it up with our teaching. But, of course, students bring an incredible array of assets into our classrooms, from their knowledge and skills to their diverse life experiences and cultural capital. The 2020 global pandemic brought to the fore the importance of creating a sense of community in our classrooms, and I believe that teaching strategies that help students feel like they belong in our classrooms provide the most effective route to the cultivation of such community.

The major revisions of these two chapters are the most substantial changes you will find in the book. But you'll find plenty of other changes along the way, including a slight re-ordering of the book's chapters, an expansion of the book's research foundation, and the addition of many new small teaching strategies. Chapter Nine, which has been re-named from "Expanding" to "Learning," provides you with an updated set of resources to continue your own growth as a teacher. I hope that these resources will enable and inspire you to move beyond the models of the book and develop your own small teaching strategies, ones that work for your specific teaching context and your unique communities of students.

I considered one final change to the book that I ultimately did not adopt. The concept of small teaching, as I explain in the introduction, was first suggested to me by watching two versions of an American sport: professional baseball and amateur softball. For this edition, I thought long and hard about coming up with an alternative way to explain the concept of small teaching for two reasons. First, the book has reached a global audience, and an analogy from an American sport might not resonate with international readers unfamiliar with baseball. This problem was brought to the fore for me as I was speaking with one of the book's translators, who was struggling to find the right way to express the concept for a translated edition. Second, many academics have little interest in sports, and might find the parallels between teaching and baseball less than compelling. I'm not the most passionate sports fan in the world, but I do enjoy watching big games in a few sports and am happy to chat about them with friends and colleagues. One of my friends on the faculty, by contrast, rolls her eyes and heads back to her office anytime the subject of what she calls "sportsball" gets raised in a hallway conversation.

While I don't want to exclude readers like her from connecting with the original conception of small teaching, it can't be denied that observing my daughter's softball games in the summer of 2014, and then watching the World Series games in the fall of 2014 was what helped to transform my journal entry from January 2014 into a fully conceived book. Both experiences demonstrated to me that small changes could have a big impact, and inspired me to see the book through to completion. Thus, you'll still find in the introduction the same explanation of the concept of small teaching that you found in the original, even with its descriptions of "sportsball" games which may have long since faded from memory (unless, of course, you are a fan of the Kansas City Royals). Readers of the first edition might notice, however, that the opening story of the "Prediction" chapter has been changed, and no longer describes the "learning" impact of informal wagering on sports games. I thought the story of my wife's remote kindergarten class introduced the concept of that chapter just as effectively and placed it more squarely within a teaching and learning context.

From my journal entry through the first edition and into this second edition, the core conviction of this book remains the same: we can improve teaching and learning by attending to the small, everyday decisions we make as we design our courses, engage in classroom practice, and communicate with students. I have seen the power of this approach to transform the lives of both teachers and students, and invite you to join me in the work.

Small Teaching

"Much of what we've been doing as teachers and students isn't serving us well, but some comparatively simple changes could make a big difference." (p. 9)

Make It Stick: The Science of Successful Learning

I n October 2014, fans of Major League Baseball relished the sight of the plucky Kansas City Royals fighting their way to the final game of the World Series. What captured the attention of so many baseball enthusiasts was that the key to the Royals' success throughout the season had been an old-fashioned approach to the sport called small ball. Rather than relying on muscle-bound sluggers hitting grand slams, the Royals instead utilized the simple, incremental strategies that enable baseball teams to move runners from one base to the next and keep the other team from scoring: bunting, stealing bases, hitting sacrifice fly balls, and playing solid defense. These unglamorous achievements on the field don't win baseball players the accolades that they might earn from smashing game-winning home runs, but teams who play small ball in concerted and effective ways don't need those kinds of dramatic heroics. Indeed, some baseball analysts pointed to the success of the Royals, who achieved their victories on a relatively small budget, as evidence of the future of baseball. "The Royals have found a winning formula," wrote Sean

Gregory, the baseball columnist for *Time* magazine. "These days, if you swing for the fences, you're more likely than ever to strike out. So just put the ball in play. . .and take your chances with your legs. Steal bases to eke out those diminishing runs. Small-ball is cheap and effective. This is where the game is headed" (Gregory 2014b). As the article notes, the wonderful feature of small ball is that it's both effective and inexpensive—and hence available to everyone. Even teams that spend money on those high-profile sluggers can still play small ball—as was evidenced in the final game of the World Series, in which the bigger-budget San Francisco Giants snatched victory from the Royals by beating them at their own game and scoring two of their three runs on unglamorous sacrifice fly balls (Gregory 2014a).

My own acquaintance with small ball comes from a less dramatic story than the one the Kansas City Royals engineered in fall 2014. I have five children and live in a New England city where love for baseball runs deep. For 15 years I sat on uncomfortable metal benches for 2 months every late spring and watched my children play various levels of softball and baseball in our city leagues. The particular league to which my children belonged was a longstanding one; many of the coaches played in the league when they were children. These coaches frequently took the games quite seriously, perhaps in an effort to recapture the glory of their childhood playing days. As a result, they scouted and selected the best players every year who were coming up from the younger leagues and thus left newer or inexperienced coaches to draft their teams from a much depleted talent pool. Yet, despite the advantages that these more aggressive coaches gained in recruiting the top players, they didn't always win. In little league as in the major leagues, the coaches who seemed to have the greatest success were the ones who focused their attention—and the attention of their players—on mastering all of the small elements of the game. Small-ball coaches would signal their base runners to steal when the fielders were haphazardly tossing the ball around the infield, or they would ensure that someone was always backing up a throw to first base in case the first-base person dropped the ball. Since nobody was bashing home runs out of the park on a softball team of 8-year-olds, small ball represented the only guaranteed strategy for long-term success in these youth leagues.

The idea for this book began to percolate at the end of one of those long softball seasons, as I was preparing for a round of fall visits to other college campuses in support of my previous book, *Cheating Lessons*, which was focused on how we can reduce cheating and promote academic integrity in higher education. When I first began giving presentations on this topic, I relished the chance to speak to my fellow college and university teachers about major transformations they could make to their courses. Unfortunately, I was usually making such visits during the middle of a semester, which meant that workshop participants had to wait until the following semester to implement any of my suggestions. Even instructors with the best of intentions to revitalize their teaching might find it challenging to carry what they had learned in a two-hour workshop in October to their course planning in January or August, given all the work that would occupy their minds in the interim. More fundamentally, sudden and dramatic transformation to one's teaching is hard work and can prove a tough sell to instructors with so many time-consuming responsibilities. As a working instructor myself, I teach courses in literature and writing every semester, so I know full well the depth of this challenge. As much as I frequently feel the urge to shake up my teaching practices with radical new innovations, I mostly don't. Reconceiving your courses from the ground up takes time and energy that most of us have in short supply in the middle of the semester, and that we usually expend on our research or service work during the semester breaks.

My reflections on this dilemma led me to consider whether I should incorporate into my workshops more activities that instructors could turn around and use in their classrooms the next morning or the next week without an extensive overhaul of their teaching—the pedagogical equivalents, in other words, of small ball. With that prospect in mind, I dove into the literature of teaching and learning in higher education with new eyes, seeking small-ball recommendations that were both easy to implement and well-supported by the research. Over the course of many months this search led me through the work of cognitive psychologists who study the mechanics of learning, to neuroscientists and biologists who helped me understand some basic aspects of brain science, and to research in learning-related fields such as emotions and motivation. I was pleasantly surprised to find in these fields a manageable number of learning principles that seemed readily translatable into higher education classrooms. Gradually I began searching for practical examples of how these principles could operate in the classroom, and I began recommending some of the strategies I was discovering to participants in my workshops. I could feel the energy and excitement rising in the room whenever participants could see a short road between a late afternoon workshop and a concrete and positive change that they could make in their classes the next morning. But nothing made me more interested and excited than the small successes I experienced when I incorporated some of the strategies I had learned about into my own classroom. Over the course of that fall semester, as I both worked on my own teaching and spoke with other instructors about these ideas, I became convinced of the seemingly paradoxical notion that fundamental pedagogical improvement was possible through incremental change—in the same way that winning the World Series was possible through stealing bases and hitting sacrifice fly balls.

This newfound conviction ultimately gave rise to the notion of *small teaching*, an approach that seeks to spark positive change in higher education through small but powerful modifications to our course design and teaching practices. Small teaching as a fully developed strategy draws from the deep well of research on learning and higher education to create a deliberate, structured, and incremental approach to changing our courses for the better. The past several decades have brought us a growing body of research on how human beings learn, and a new generation of scholars in those fields has begun to translate findings from the laboratories of memory and cognition researchers to the higher education classrooms of today. Their findings increasingly suggest the potency of small shifts in how we design our courses, conduct our classrooms, and communicate with our students. Some of the findings may also suggest pathways to change that arise from dramatic transformation to our courses, and I applaud those innovators who are pointing us down those routes. But if we are seeking to boost our students' learning of course content, to improve their basic intellectual skills—such as writing, speaking, and critical thinking—and to prepare them for success in their careers, then I believe we can find in small teaching an approach to our shared work of educating students that is effective for our students and accessible to the largest number of working college and university teachers.

Widespread accessibility to working teachers matters a great deal, especially if we consider the incredibly diverse range of contexts in which higher education operates these days. Teaching innovations that have the potential to spur broad changes must be as accessible to underpaid and overworked adjuncts as they are to tenured faculty at research universities. They must find a home on the campus of a small liberal arts college as easily as they do on the commuter campuses of regional comprehensives. They must offer something to traditional lecturers in big rooms and to discussion leaders in small seminars. They should be as available to us in ordinary times as they are in the midst of a pandemic. The activities outlined in this book, taken as a whole, fulfill these directives: with a little bit of creative thinking, they can translate into every conceivable type of teaching environment in higher education, from lectures in cavernous classrooms to discussions in small seminar rooms, from fully face-to-face to fully online courses and every blended shade between. They stem from very basic principles of how human beings learn and hence cross both discipline and content type—whether you are teaching students to memorize facts or formulae, to develop their speaking or writing skills, or to solve complex and wicked problems. Not every instructor in every discipline in every teaching context will find a space for all of the small teaching activities outlined here, but every reader should find opportunities to use at least some of them. You can implement them tomorrow morning, next week on Friday, in the design of your next quiz or test, and even in the next e-mail you send to your students.

To ensure that these techniques lent themselves to this kind of universal accessibility, and thus merit space beneath the umbrella of small teaching, the principles outlined in this book had to meet three basic criteria. First, they had to have some foundation in the learning sciences. Fortunately, over the past decade or two a cohort of learning scientists has begun to present findings from those disciplines in forms that are accessible to nonspecialists like me. Books like Daniel Schacter's *The Seven Sins of Memory*; Daniel Willingham's *Why Don't Students Like School*; or Peter Brown, Henry Roediger, and Mark McDaniel's *Make It Stick* describe the results of research in neuroscience and cognitive theory in ways that spell out their implications clearly for teachers and learners. Since the publication of the first edition of the book, the roster of such books has only continued to expand. Notable recent titles include Patrice M. Bain and Pooja K. Agarwal's *Powerful Teaching: Unleash the Science of Learning*; Yana Weinstein, Megan Sumeracki, and Oliver Caviglioli's *Understanding How We Learn: A Visual Guide*; and Joshua R. Eyler's *How Humans Learn: The Science and Stories Behind Effective College Teaching*. All of these authors helped me identify prospective principles for the first edition of the book, and consider some new ones for this second edition.

The principles I selected almost all have solid support from experimental research of one kind or another; they emerge from the labs of neuroscientists, biologists, and psychologists. But in order for a principle to earn a spot as one of the book's chapter titles, it had to meet a second criteria: there had to be at least some research demonstrating that it could have a positive impact outside of the laboratory, in real-world educational environments— higher education–whenever possible. In other words, I had to see published accounts of experiments or qualitative research that demonstrated that this principle could make a demonstrable positive difference to student learning, performance, retention, or well-being. This test proved the most challenging one to meet; some strategies that seemed plausible to me, or that stemmed from fascinating laboratory experiments, did not ultimately make it into the book since they could not clear this essential hurdle.

Finally, I had to observe the principles directly myself somehow, either from my own experiences as a teacher or learner or from direct observation of other teaching and learning environments. Call me overly cautious, but I needed these principles to pass this final smell test for me to be absolutely certain that I could recommend them to working instructors. Most of the chapters that follow begin with an example of how I have sniffed out these principles in some learning experience from my own life or from the lives of my students or even my children, and I hope these personal examples might help you identify moments in which you have seen them at work in your own learning histories as well.

Assuming a teaching and learning activity met all three of these criteria, it still had to be capable of implementation in ways that fell under the umbrella of small teaching. As you will find in the pages that follow, a small teaching approach or activity may take one of three forms:

Brief (5–10-minute) classroom or online learning activities. I love the idea of small interventions in a learning session that can capture (or recapture) the attention of students, provide quick opportunities for student engagement, and introduce or seal up new learning. Even when you have an otherwise busy class session planned, you can find time for a five-minute activity that will provide a substantive boost to the learning of your students.

One-time interventions in a course. As in the case of the Minute Thesis exercise in Chapter Four, the meaning of *small* will occasionally shift from "a small portion of a class" to "a small portion of the course." In other words, some small teaching activities could occupy an entire class period but need to do so only one or two times in the semester.

Small modifications in course design or communication with your students. These recommendations might not translate directly into 10-minute or one-time activities, but they also do not require radical rethinking of your courses. They might inspire tweaks or small changes in the way you organize the daily schedule of your course, write your course description or assignment sheets, or respond to the writing of your students. The strategies in Part III especially will fit under this category of small teaching approaches.

An essential shared quality of all three of these forms of small teaching is that they *require minimal preparation and grading*. Although we are all busy, this feature of small teaching strikes me as especially important for adjunct instructors, who may be teaching multiple courses on different campuses or working additional jobs to make ends meet. An adjunct instructor who can walk into class every day with a variety of small teaching exercises can actually reduce overall preparation time by seeding these powerful learning activities throughout her teaching. One-time activities like the Minute Thesis or a mindful practice session, which likewise require minimal preparation or grading, can also serve as a back pocket technique that an instructor could use on a day when a sick child or medical emergency or mental health day has reduced or eliminated normal preparation time.

Yet such activities, which may first find their way into your classroom as a means of filling an empty 10 minutes at the end of class or an unplanned course session, have the power to produce as much or more learning than your anxiously overprepared lecture. For me, this represents the real power and promise of small teaching. I hope the chapters that follow will demonstrate to you that small teaching is not a realist's compromise, an inferior choice we have to make because we don't have the time or energy to make the big changes that would *really* make a difference to our students. We have excellent evidence for the learning power of small teaching activities—in study after study—as you will see in the chapters that follow. Small teaching activities have been proven to raise student performance on learning tasks by the equivalent of a full letter grade or higher. That's powerful evidence—as powerful as anything I have seen in the learning research, including in studies devoted to grand slam approaches that grab the headlines of the *Chronicle of Higher Education* or other publications of our profession.

In further service to the argument that small and incremental approaches can have great power (and to the fact that we are all busy), you will find a variety of levels at which you can understand the small teaching strategies recommended in each chapter. You will have the richest understanding of any given small teaching approach by reading the chapter in its entirety, of course, but you can also drop into the practical application sections in the latter half of the chapters if you are looking for fast and immediate help. The structure of each chapter includes the following elements:

- **Introduction:** You will usually find here examples of how the particular learning phenomenon described in that chapter might appear in everyday life.
- **In Theory:** This section delves into the research that supports the recommendations of the chapter and includes descriptions of experiments from laboratories and classrooms as well as brief descriptions of key findings or principles from the cognitive sciences.
- **Models:** Four or five detailed models are described in each chapter—fully fleshed-out examples of how instructors could incorporate a small teaching approach into their course design, classroom or online practice, or communication with students. This second edition contains a number of new models that I have encountered since the book's initial publication.
- **Principles:** I hope and expect that instructors will not simply follow the models, but also will take the overall strategy and develop their own new models. The principles provide guidance for creating your own small teaching strategies.
- **Quick Tips:** One-sentence reminders of the simplest means of putting the small teaching strategies of that chapter into practice; flip through or return to these when you have 15 minutes before class and need a quick tip for an engaged learning activity.
- **Conclusion:** A final reflection on the main theory or strategy of the chapter.

I hope that your first reading of each chapter will help you see immediately how to make changes to your teaching that will benefit your students. But I hope as well that you can continue to rely on the book long after your first reading. Keep it handy and flip through it every now and again or whenever you feel the need to try something new and different in your classroom. Use the book to spark new or newly invigorated conversations on your campus about how we can best help our students learn and about how we can best promote positive change in higher education. Finally, when you are ready to further explore the literature on teaching and learning in higher education, and move beyond these specific recommendations, review the reading suggestions in Chapter Nine for more ideas. I have attempted to keep the references in the chapters as spare as possible, in order not to overwhelm new readers to this field or force them to hunt down articles in specialized journals. Throughout the book I sought to support my claims about small teaching, whenever possible, by pointing readers to accessible books that offer good analyses or overviews of the research on human learning.

The small teaching models and principles that you will find in the chapters ahead can be taken singly, as one-time spurs to innovation in a specific course session or unit plan, but they could also be combined to create an entirely new approach to your teaching. If you are reading this book over a break, while you are not teaching, see if you can draw systematically from each of the three major parts of the book as you plan your next course, creating a comprehensive strategy for boosting student learning in your classroom. But if you are reading it during the middle of the semester, shift your focus from the forest to the trees. Select one activity or course modification, and commit to it for the rest of the semester. Make sure you give new activities time to flower; nothing works exactly as we might hope it would on the first attempt, so it might take several iterations before activities like opening or closing prediction exercises really begin to pay dividends. And as I will argue in the conclusion, search for ways to evaluate the effects of your small teaching changes and determine whether they belong in your permanent teaching repertoire. Enlist the help of the teaching and learning center on your campus, if you have one, to help you better understand how to measure the impact of specific changes to your teaching on student learning. Students are not the only ones who will benefit from new learning as the result of small teaching, in other words; you can use these activities to take a more systematic approach to your own teaching, thinking deliberately about implementing, measuring, and modifying a range of possible teaching strategies in ways that will keep you learning and growing as a teacher throughout your career.

But we shouldn't get too far ahead of ourselves, and worry yet about your whole career. I will assume that you have class tomorrow, or next Monday, or at least within the next month or two, and you're looking for ideas.

Let's start small.

Part I

Knowledge

I magine the media storm that erupted in 1956 upon the publication of an educational book with the attention-grabbing title of *Taxonomy of Educational Objectives: The Classification of Educational Goals, Handbook I: Cognitive Domain*. The author of this spine tingler was psychologist Benjamin Bloom, who sought to articulate a set of objectives that teachers could use to guide their instructional activities. In spite of its eye-glazing title, the book's content ultimately became a sacred text for educational theorists and administrators everywhere, giving them both a conceptual framework and a vocabulary to articulate what they expected learners could achieve in their classrooms. The taxonomy that Bloom created contains six major categories: Knowledge, Comprehension, Application, Analysis, Synthesis, and Evaluation. A quick glance over the six categories would suggest that they follow a progression from lower to higher orders of complexity, from a static possession of knowledge to more creative forms of thinking in the categories of synthesis and evaluation. Indeed, the taxonomy is often depicted in the shape of a pyramid, with knowledge at the bottom and evaluation or creation at the apex.

Unfortunately, this visual image of Bloom's taxonomy as a pyramid, which all teachers have likely encountered at some point in their lives, has led many higher education instructors to view Bloom's categories in a distorted way. When you think of a pyramid, after all, where do you want to be? At the top, of course. Nobody wants to be down on the bottom row of a pyramid, crushed by the weight of the rising layers, unable to reach for the cognitive stars. So some instructors seem to believe that the learning of facts or concepts, or helping students remember facts and concepts—or even procedures or basic skills—falls beneath them; they are interested only in higher order activities like critical thinking or making judgments or creating new knowledge. College instructors seem especially prone to this desire to hop over the bottom layer of the pyramid—or, more charitably, to assume either that elementary and secondary educators should have helped students learn how to remember things or that students should master knowledge outside of class and class time can be exclusively devoted to higher cognitive activities. In recent years such instructors have used a new argument to justify their dismissal of the knowledge category of Bloom's taxonomy: the omnipresence of search engines. Why should we bother to help students remember facts, so this argument runs, when all of the facts of the entire world are available to them at the touch of a fingertip? Facts now come in the form of smartphones. Let the Internet provide students with the facts, and we will instead focus our energies on the higher cognitive activities that make use of those facts.

Appealing though it might be to offload the responsibility for teaching our students basic knowledge to their elementary school teachers or to Google™, the research of cognitive psychologists who study learning and the basic study habits of most students suggest that we cannot do this. One of our first and most important tasks as teachers is to help students develop a rich body of knowledge in our content areas—without doing so, we diminish considerably their ability to engage in cognitive activities like thinking and evaluating and creating. As cognitive psychologist Daniel Willingham has argued, you can't think creatively about information unless you have information in your head to think about. "Research from cognitive science has shown," he explains, "that the sorts of skills that teachers want for their students—such as the ability to analyze and think critically—*require* extensive factual knowledge" (Willingham 2014, p. 25). We have to know things, in other words, to think critically about them. Without any information readily available to use in our brains, we tend to see new facts (from our Internet searches) in isolated, noncontextual ways that lead to shallow thinking. Facts are related to other facts, and the more of those relationships we can see, the more we will prove capable of critical analysis and creative thinking. Students who don't bother to memorize anything will never get much beyond skating over the surface of a topic.

But the issue runs more deeply than this. When we learn new facts, we are building up mental structures that enable us to process and organize the next set of new facts more effectively. Knowledge is foundational: we won't have the structures in place to do deep thinking if we haven't spent time mastering a body of knowledge related to that thinking. The depiction of Bloom's taxonomy as a pyramid actually does acknowledge this important principle; one cannot get to the top levels of creative and critical thinking without a broad and solid foundation of knowledge beneath them. As Willingham puts it, "Thinking well requires knowing facts, and that's true not simply because you need something to think *about*. The very processes that teachers care most about—critical thinking processes such as reasoning and problem-solving—are intimately intertwined with factual knowledge that is stored in long-term memory (not just found in the environment)" (Willingham 2014, p. 28).

In his book *Curious,* Ian Leslie argues that such knowledge is "the hidden power" of our cognition (Leslie 2015, p. 121); the more of it we have, the more deeply we can think.

As a simple illustration of the intertwinement of facts and thinking, consider the example of a lawyer who has to build an argument over the course of a trial, responding on short notice to witnesses or actions by the judge. We might think about a lawyer who works skillfully in such a situation as an adept and creative thinker, one who can respond quickly on her feet and construct arguments with facility. But if we listen to her making those arguments, we are likely to hear lots and lots of facts: legal principles, examples from other famous cases, statements from other witnesses, and so on. Undoubtedly, the lawyer in this case demonstrates complex cognitive and creative skills in building arguments from facts, but no such thinking will arise without those facts. More important, the lawyer's gradual mastery of a body of facts, over the course of years of study and legal practice, enables her to take what she is encountering in this trial and invest it with meaning by connecting it with previous cases and trials, thus better preparing her for her next round of critical thinking in the courtroom. Likewise, I know that if I ask students to think critically about the meaning of a Romantic poem in my literature survey course, the student with a deep factual knowledge of the historical context in which it was written will offer me a better analysis than the one who just eyeballs it and Googles™ a few facts at random. We need factual material in our memory for every cognitive skill we might want to teach our students.

We should not assume that students are either willing or capable of mastering such foundational knowledge on their own, in their study and learning outside of the classroom. In fact, research on student learning strategies suggests that students typically make poor choices when they attempt to learn new information— and that they make those choices even when they know better.

Brown, Roediger, and McDaniel, the authors of *Make it Stick: The Science of Successful Learning*, describe a fascinating experiment in which students were given two different strategies for learning how to identify characteristics of the work of different painters: studying the paintings either in similar groups (i.e., *massed* studying) or all mixed together (i.e., *interleaved* studying). The students who studied the paintings in interleaved fashion performed better on tests they took after their study periods—but this did not seem to make a difference in how they thought about studying, as the authors explain: "Despite [the] results, the students who participated in these experiments persisted in preferring massed practice, convinced that it served them better. Even after they took the test and could have realized from their own performance that interleaving was the better strategy for learning, they clung to their belief that the concentrated viewing of paintings by one artist was better" (Brown, Roediger, and McDaniel 2014, p. 54). In other words, these students continued to believe in the superior power of a study strategy that had just been demonstrated to them as less effective than a simple alternative.

Like all of us, these students suffered from biases and misconceptions about learning and how it works. Tell students to study for a test, and most of them will pull out their notebooks or textbooks and read them over and over again, despite scads of research telling us that this is just about the least effective learning strategy for mastering a new body of information. Even if students have encountered this research or have been taught effective study strategies by previous teachers, they still are likely to persist in ineffective learning strategies.

Hence, if we care about students having knowledge that they can use to practice their higher order cognitive skills, we should help them acquire that knowledge. We might rightly not want to spend an extraordinary amount of time and energy on this aspect of their learning, which is what makes it such a perfect realm for small teaching. As you will read in what follows, small teaching activities in the realm of prediction, retrieval, and interleaving can all provide significant boosts to your students' mastery of foundational knowledge and skills. Such activities, leveraged into the first and final minutes of a class session, can provide a powerful boost to student mastery of knowledge; so, too, can simple tweaks to the organization of your course and the order in which you introduce new material and review older material. Taking advantage of these easy opportunities to help students remember course material will ensure that students can engage more deeply and meaningfully in the complex learning tasks to which you want to devote more of your time and energy—and to which we give more full consideration in Part Two.

Chapter 1

Predicting

INTRODUCTION

My wife, Anne, teaches kindergarten, and during the 2020–2021 school year she taught it remotely from our dining room. Whenever you find it challenging to maintain the focus of your students, you should envision attempting to corral the attention of a couple of dozen five-year-olds through your computer screen and feel just a little bit better about your prospects. I was working from home as well during the pandemic, and so I had the pleasure (I think) of overhearing almost everything she did with her students all day long. I hummed along to the songs she sang about the weather and days of the week, counted my way to one hundred by ones and fives and tens, and listened to her patiently introduce letters and syllables and words to her students.

At some point every day she would read a picture book to the faces gathered on her screen, and this process always started in the same way. She would display the cover of the book, read aloud the title, and then ask her students some variation of the following question: "What do you think this book is going to be about?" She would then pose additional questions based on the specifics of the picture and the title. "What do you think will happen if you give a mouse a cookie?" "What would it be like to take a polar bear for a walk?" A final set of questions was designed to surface whatever students already knew about the subject matter of the book: "Where do polar bears live? Are polar bears pets?" The students would sing out their answers, some of which were on target and some of which were not. (Polar bears do NOT make good pets.) But almost always the process of reading a story aloud to the students began with a few minutes of these efforts by the students to make some predictions about what would unfold in the story they were about to hear.

In higher education we tend to go into class with our content guns blazing: I HAVE SOME STUFF TO TEACH YOU, LET'S GET STARTED! But the research on human learning that we will consider in this chapter suggests that the first step in the learning process should be to follow Anne's lead—not necessarily through her specific activity of asking pre-reading questions–but by asking students to engage in predictive activities of some kind or another *before* we expose them to new course content. Such activities could include inviting students to answer questions about what they are about to learn or experience, but could also include asking students to solve problems that are beyond their current ability level or to try their hand at a new skill before they have been given any formal instruction. This approach can seem counterintuitive since it turns the normal teaching sequence on its head. The operating assumption of many teachers runs like this: *First* I teach them the material, *then* I have them answer questions or solve problems with it. Read the story about polar bears, and then ask them where polar bears live. Give students a lecture on poetry, and then have them interpret a poem. Show students how to solve a particular type of math problem, and then give them one to solve on their own. But learning research suggests something quite different. It tells us that asking students to use their existing knowledge and skills to struggle with the material *before* we teach it can provide a robust foundation for deeper learning.

Providing opportunities for students to undertake this struggle doesn't take much time or effort, which is why it makes an ideal place to start a book on small teaching: just a few min-utes at the beginning of a class period or a unit or even a course has enormous potential to improve both student learning and your teaching.

IN THEORY

To understand how and why predictive activities support learning, consider first an elegant series of experiments conducted by three researchers at UCLA (Kornell, Jenson Hayes, and Bjork 2009). The authors asked subjects in one of these experiments to memorize a series of loosely connected word pairs, such as *whale–mammal*. One group of the subjects was given 13 seconds to study each word pair; the other group was given 8 seconds to see only the first word and to make a prediction about the second, after which they had 5 seconds to see the full word pair. Since the second word of the pair was linked to the first, but only one of many possibilities (since you might well guess *sea* or *ocean* or *large* if you saw only the word *whale*), participants typically guessed the second half of the pair incorrectly. Note also that the subjects in the second (prediction) group had only 5 seconds to view the correct answer, so 8 seconds less than those in the first (nonprediction) group. Yet in spite of this shorter study time, and in spite of the fact that subjects in the second group frequently predicted the second half of the word pair incorrectly, the subjects in the second group performed significantly better than those in the first group when they were asked to recollect the word pairs on a subsequent exam: 67% accu-racy in the second group versus 55% in the first. The unsuccess-ful prediction attempts in the experimental group, the authors explain, "were, remarkably, more effective than was spending the same time studying the answer to be recalled later" (p. 994). In other words, taking a few seconds to predict the answer before learning it, *even when the prediction was incorrect*, seemed to increase subsequent retention of learned material. This was true even when that prediction time substituted for—rather than supplemented— more conventional forms of studying.

The results of laboratory experiments like this one prompted another group of researchers, led by cognitive psychologist Elizabeth Bjork, to see whether they could reproduce the positive learning effect of prediction in an actual classroom (Carey 2014b). The researchers gave students in Bjork's introductory psychology class short multiple-choice pretests before some of the lectures in her course. Since the pretest questions asked them about material that had not yet been covered, the students performed about as well on the pretests as they would have from guessing randomly— again, as in the laboratory experiment, they made plenty of wrong predictions. Lectures on the subject matter followed immediately after the pretests, so the students received quick feedback on their answers. At the end of the term, the students took a final exam that contained multiple-choice questions similar to the ones on the pretests. The results paralleled the results of the laboratory experiment almost exactly: students performed around 10% better on questions from the subject areas in which they had been pretested than on those on which they had not. Bjork concluded from this experiment that "giving students a pretest on topics to be covered in a lecture improves their ability to answer related questions about those topics on a later final exam" (Carey 2014b). Note, of course, that even though the vocabulary has changed slightly here—from *prediction* to *pretesting*—the cognitive activity is similar: asking learners to give answers to questions or anticipate outcomes about which they do not yet have sufficient information or understanding. They are trying before they are ready.

Before we explore the reasons that prediction boosts learning, consider one final example of prediction in higher education, this one from an online environment (Ogan, Aleven, and Jones 2009).

Three researchers from Carnegie Mellon University developed an online tutoring program that demonstrated the power of predicting in helping students improve their intercultural understanding in hybrid language courses. The two French courses described in the experiment each met once a week in a face-to-face environment, but otherwise the students did their course work online. Part of the goal for these courses was to help students develop what the authors called "intercultural competence, that is, the ability to think and act in culturally appropriate ways" (p. 268). This can be an extremely difficult skill to develop, as anyone who has ever traveled in a foreign country can likely attest. The ability to speak the language of a foreign country does not necessarily guarantee your ability to understand how to hail a cab, tip in a restaurant, or approach a stranger in the Paris Metro to ask which train will take you to the airport in time to catch your flight home (as I once discovered, to my great sorrow). So, in this experiment we are moving beyond the realm of simply knowing and retaining information into the broader realm of comprehension—that is, understanding how to use and apply in other contexts the information you have learned. The intercultural competence sought by these instructors requires learners to think and act with their knowledge, not just report it back.

To help students acquire this type of deeper comprehension, two experts in computer-assisted learning worked with a language professor to develop an online tutoring program based on the use of film clips. In the control condition of this experiment, students were shown film clips highlighting cultural attitudes or behaviors that are normally taught in introductory French classes. As the students watched the short film clips, they had the opportunity to take notes on what they saw. The students in the experimental group, by contrast, were given the opportunity to use the power of prediction to improve their learning. Their film clips would pause at key moments, ask them to make a prediction about what was about to unfold, and then require them to ponder what actually happened once the clip had finish: the authors described their three-part sequence with the catchy phrase *pause–predict–ponder*. The prediction the students had to make actually came from a drop-down menu of choices, but then they had open text boxes to explain why they made that prediction. After they had watched the remainder of the clip, they had to answer a simple question about whether or not their prediction was correct and then respond to prompts to help them reflect on their prediction, such as: "If so [i.e., if your prediction was correct], did you see anything you didn't expect about the French culture? If not, what happened that you didn't predict?" Students in both conditions concluded their viewing of the film clips with required postings to a discussion board to allow them to process and review what they had seen.

After the class, the researchers looked at two different measures to see whether the pause–predict–ponder exercises had improved student mastery of intercultural competence: student scores on tests of cultural knowledge, and their more general cultural thinking or reasoning skills through their discussion board posts. The students who had the opportunity to make predictions outscored their peers on the first exam by about that same 10% margin that we saw in the earlier experiments, with some diminishing returns on the subsequent assignments—which might tell us that prediction, like many of the active learning interventions we will consider in this book, especially helps new learners. Ratings of the posts in the discussion board also showed the students in the experimental condition performing significantly higher on assessments of intercultural competence than those in the control condition. In the discussion of their results, the researchers note that students made correct predictions only about 40% of the time, another point in favor of the notion (to be qualified shortly) that wrong predictions do no harm. They also point to an interesting side benefit they witnessed: students in the experimental condition posted more frequently on the discussion boards, and more frequently on target, than those in the control condition: "The experimental group showed a better ability to maintain a productive discussion compared to the control group (p. 283)." It seems that in this case the prediction activity also helped engage the students more thoroughly in the material.

Researchers who study the brain can help clarify the mechanics that underpin the results of all of these experiments. Neuroscientists are increasingly demonstrating that our brains are prediction-making machines, and that our learning stems most fundamentally from the cycle of making predictions and then adjusting our thinking in light of the accuracy of those predictions. Stanislas Dehaene is a professor of experimental cognitive psychology at the College de France, and the Director of the Neurospin Brain Imaging Center. In his book *How We Learn: Why Brains Learn Better Than Any Machine . . . for Now*, he offers a detailed but accessible tour of learning and the brain, and concludes that "Generating a prediction, detecting one's error, and correcting oneself are the very foundation of effective learning" (Dehaene 2020, p. 209). Our brains continuously create models of the world around us, use those models to predict how our experiences will unfold, and engage in corrective re-modeling in light of what actually happens. That corrective re-modeling is what we call learning. A new driver's brain makes continuous predictions about how the car will behave as she drives—she expects the car to slow down and come to a stop when she brakes. The first time she drives in the snow, applies the brake, and finds herself skidding, her brain notes the failure of her existing mental model—applying the brakes doesn't *always* stop the car with the same efficacy. She has to take weather conditions into account. Her mental model of driving expands, her predictive abilities as a driver improve. She has learned.

In a classroom setting, predictive activities reveal to students the gaps and problems in their existing knowledge of the course subject matter and provoke them to fill and repair their understanding. When I am asked to make a prediction or try a new skill, I am forced to surface whatever knowledge and skills I currently possess and use them in service of the task in front of me. In some cases, I will see immediately that I don't have what I need—*I have no idea how to do this*, I might think to myself. In a classroom setting, that recognition should push me toward learning: *If I want to succeed in here, I need more information.* But I might equally well think I *do* have enough information or skill to get the job done, in which case I will make a confident prediction, assuming that I already know everything I need to know. When I discover that my prediction was incorrect, I am put back on my heels again. What went wrong? What information was I missing? What would I have needed to know in order to get it right? Since very few students, if any, will come into our classes knowing everything they need to know already, the predictive activities we design are likely to reveal at least some errors in their thinking, showing them the gaps in their knowledge and skills. Ideally, your course material then gives them precisely what they need in order to fill those gaps.

Predictive activities can also give students a clearer understanding of what and how they need to study and learn in any particular course. As Elizabeth Bjork points out in relation to the practice tests in her experiments, "Taking a practice test and getting answers wrong seems to improve subsequent study, because the test adjusts our thinking in some way to the kind of material we need to know" (quoted in Carey 2014b). Well-planned pretests or predictive activities alert the students to essential course content and the testing style of the instructor. Envision a student sitting in a chemistry course in the fall semester of her first year of college. She had a year of chemistry in high school, and her high school teacher focused entirely on having students memorize facts and formulae, knowledge of which he assessed exclusively through multiple-choice tests. She has been conditioned by that teacher to think about and learn chemistry through rote learning, a memorization technique she will carry into her new course—unless, of course, her college professor opens the semester by asking the class to try to answer some conceptual questions, and mentions that these problems are similar to ones that will appear on the final exam. When that first-year student finds herself scratching her head and unable to come up with the answers, she will immediately see that she has to approach this course, and her learning, in a new way. She has to focus on conceptual understanding instead of the memorization of facts. If she hadn't encountered that first-day predictive activity, she might have spent the first five weeks of the semester, before the first major exam, focused entirely on repeating her high school study practices.

Ultimately and perhaps most simply, predictive activities mimic something we normally ask of learners who are attempting to master a skill: requiring them to *try before they are ready*. We can all likely draw from our experiences with attempts to master skills of one sort or another, and we know full well that however much one might read in advance about throwing a football or painting a portrait or giving a speech, the real learning happens after we have thrown ourselves into the situation and made that first (unsuccessful) attempt. When I took a class to become licensed in scuba diving, we spent the first half of every session in a classroom taking notes on some skill we would have to practice in the pool. I typically jumped in the pool for the second half of class thinking I had that skill mastered, but within a few minutes the gaps in my knowledge were revealed, and I floundered around for a while, doing it completely wrong until the instructor swam over and gave me the help I needed, at which point the real learning began.

We facilitate this type of learning in many academic contexts, asking students to try out cognitive skills before they are ready. I don't spend the entire semester lecturing to my freshman composition students about all of the writing techniques they will need to write a perfect academic essay and then give them one final assignment to show me how they have mastered those skills. I assign essays from the beginning of the semester, even though some of what they need to write great academic essays won't be covered for another 4 or 8 or 12 weeks. Asking students to make predictions before learning new material just represents another version of this common teaching approach.

MODELS

The ideal grounds for small teaching activities related to prediction are the openings of a learning experience—a course, a learning unit, a class period. Consider the following models for leveraging predicting into the beginning of anything you might be teaching.

Activating Prior Knowledge

Engaging in an act of prediction begins with my rooting around in my brain for anything which I already know that will help me make a successful prediction. It requires me to tap into my existing knowledge and skills, whatever they might be. I use my existing knowledge of French culture to predict what will happen in the video, or my prior knowledge of chemistry to predict what will happen in an experiment. This *activation of prior knowledge*, as learning researchers call it, has been demonstrated as having plenty of power to boost learning. "Prior knowledge plays a critical role in learning," explain Susan Ambrose and Marsha Lovett, "which means that. . .faculty members need to assess the content, beliefs and skills students bring with them into courses and. . .use that information as both a foundation for new learning as well as an opportunity to intervene when content knowledge is inaccurate or insufficient" (Ambrose and Lovett 2014, p. 16). The easiest way to activate the prior knowledge of your students is to ask them to make individual and collective knowledge dumps, telling you everything they know—or think they know—about your subject before you begin teaching them. You might think about this as a pre-prediction activity, or a half-step toward prediction. Instead of drawing up their prior knowledge and using it to solve a new problem, students are simply drawing up that prior knowledge and showing it to you—and the research suggests that this step on its own, *even if they don't use their prior knowledge to solve a new problem,* can prepare them for deeper learning.

Our first small teaching strategy might therefore be the easiest one to implement in the book: before you teach something new to your students, ask them what they already know about it. You could do this in multiple ways that fit the frame of small teaching:

- Prior to introducing new content in a course, ask students to take a pre-quiz or respond to two or three questions about the subject matter on the course's learning management system and then summarize those results briefly at the start of the first or second class.
- At the start of any individual class period, ask students to write down what they think they already know about the subject for that day. Tell them to list three to five things they have learned in previous classes or from their life experiences, and have them pair up to compare notes. Solicit a few responses and build on them in the opening of your presentation of the new material.

- At the start of the semester, devote part of one class period to assessing students' current state of knowledge, either through whole-class or group activities or through a written pretest. Once you have heard what students have to offer in such an exercise and have gained a glimpse into their existing knowledge, you can strategize how to build upon it most effectively in the course.

As an example of the third suggestion, when I teach a seminar on twenty-first-century British literature and culture, I set aside 30 minutes on the first day of the semester for a knowledge dump in which students respond to the following question: "When I say the word *British*, what are the primary impressions that form in your mind?" I pose this question and give them a few minutes to make a list on paper, and then we fill up the board with their impressions. I try to categorize their impressions so we can see patterns—and the same basic patterns always emerge. *British* to them means the royal family, traditional activities like having tea and biscuits or taking long walks in the country, green landscapes, and ruined castles. None of them ever mention the ethnic diversity of Britain, or the fact that *Britishness* encompasses the peoples of Scotland and Wales and Northern Ireland, or its recent political history. The second class period, in which we begin considering the political and cultural context of British literature, then gives me an opportunity not to dismiss their impressions but to build upon them as I introduce features of Britishness that they have never encountered. Throughout the semester I will occasionally return to the impressions we laid out on that first day and remind them about how our current text or discussion connects back to them. Such an opening-class activity can obviously work in almost any type of course, modified in ways that best fit your inclinations. For an upper-level course you might want to narrow down the questions, since they might have more general extensive knowledge than would fit into a paragraph. The overall strategy here remains happily simple: prior to the introduction of any major new chunk of course content, spend a class period (for a whole course) or a few minutes (for a new unit) asking them what they already know.

Polling Predictions

The use of classroom polling—whether you go high-tech with programs like Poll Everywhere or low-tech with colored index cards or even just raised hands—presents a very simple route to making prediction part of your course lectures, as Derek Bruff points out in his book *Teaching with Classroom Response Systems: Creating Active Learning Environments* (Bruff 2009). His chapter "A Taxonomy of Clicker Questions" points to the power of prediction to increase comprehension in addition to the benefits it should provide in boosting memory of individual facts and concepts. For example, Bruff gives an example of a math instructor at a small college who "shows his students a graphing program that allows him to vary a parameter in a function, such as the parameter ω in the function sin (ωt), and asks his students to predict what will happen to the graph of a function when he changes that parameter. After the students vote with their clickers, he demonstrates the correct answer using his graphing program" (p. 85). Students cannot answer questions like this with simple plug-and-chug–type knowledge; they have to possess a conceptual understanding of the problem to make an accurate prediction. The failure or success of their predictions enables them to re-model that conceptual understanding, which is of course the most important learning the course should induce.

Bruff also notes that classroom polling can support the opportunity for instructors to ask students for predictions behind the screen of anonymity, which can be useful in certain contexts. He provides an example of a health and wellness course at another university in which instructors want to draw attention to student perceptions of drinking on campus. The instructors first ask the students how many alcoholic drinks they consumed at their last social occasion, but then they also ask students to predict what they think the responses of their peers will look like. "The differences between the predicted votes and the actual votes," explains Bruff, "are often surprising to students because it turns out that students are not always as risky as they think they are" (p. 86). The benefit of such a quick prediction exercise is the rich discussion that follows: "This activity can lead to a productive class-wide discussion of social perceptions of risky behavior and the role that marketing, in particular, plays in those perceptions" (p. 86). Such discussions, in other words, can encourage the students to reflect on why their predictions were incorrect—and the role that social media or beer commercials might play in driving their perceptions of their peers' consumption of alcohol. The potential screen of anonymity provided by clickers obviously can serve a useful purpose when asking students to make predictions based on their own personal behaviors. It also could prove useful anytime you feel students might not want their predictions shared publicly, either because they want something kept private or because they feel they might be embarrassed by making a wildly incorrect prediction in front of their peers (or in front of you).

Prediction–Exposure–Feedback

Even without formal testing or the use of clickers, you can always ask students to make informal, in-class predictions about any course material to which they are about to be exposed. This could happen in almost any discipline, in any type of class.

Scientists know full well how prediction plays a role in the scientific method—in the form of the hypothesis—and likely already ask students to engage in predictive activities in their use of laboratory experiments and reports. But outside of the laboratory, and in other disciplines, instructors can still follow this same basic approach. Get into the habit of asking students to make predictions about new content based on their knowledge from earlier in the semester, from their previous courses, or from their own general knowledge. *How Learning Works* gaves two quick examples of this: "Before asking students to read an article from the 1970s, you might ask them what was going on historically at the time that might have informed the author's perspective. Or when presenting students with a design problem, you might ask them how a famous designer, whose work they know, might have approached the problem." In these kinds of questions, again, you are requiring students "not only to draw on prior knowledge but also to use it to reason about new knowledge" (Ambrose, Bridges, DiPietro, Lovett, and Norman 2010, p. 33). Ideally, you will both ask for the prediction and give them the opportunity to explain why they made it; doing so will require them to examine their thinking and might help them recognize their knowledge and skill gaps. Even more ideally, after you give them the answer you might ask them to explain why their predictions did or did not hold true.

Earlier in this chapter, I described for you three experiments on learning designed to demonstrate the power of predictions. Imagine that I was describing those experiments for students in a psychology or education course. I describe the setup of the first experiment—with one group of students trying to memorize the word pairs for 13 seconds, and a second group making their guess and then seeing the correct answer for five seconds—and then stop and ask the students to predict the results. I could do this in a generic way, and just invite some students to raise their hands and speculate, or I could offer specific options and invite students to select the one they think would be correct:

- Memorizers performed 50% better on the test.
- Memorizers performed 10% better on the test.
- The two groups performed about equally.
- Predicters performed 10% better on the test.
- Predicters performed 50% better on the test.

(If all is going well in this chapter, you will remember that the answer is number four.) Students could select the answer they think was correct using polling or simply by raising their hands. After I record the student votes, I might invite a few students to explain their answers, and then show the results. After those results have been revealed, I can use them to make the two points that matter the most: prediction enhanced learning, and it did so by a small but significant margin. Once students have seen the results of this initial experiment, the next two experiments I tell them about will help confirm the knowledge that they have now lodged more firmly in their brains.

If your teaching routine includes describing surveys or experiments for your students, consider varying the typical pattern of describing the setup and then showing the results. Instead describe the setup and ask students to predict the results. After you have shown them the results, invite them to reflect upon the accuracy or inaccuracy of their predictions: Why did they get it wrong or right? What did they learn when the results were revealed?

Closing Predictions

Predictions can close a class as easily as they can open them, but in the case of closing predictions you are pointing students toward the material that they will be reading or studying for homework. Many textbooks include prediction-style questions at the beginning of a chapter; I suspect that few students read or think about those questions unless they are specifically required to do so. If you have spent a class period finishing up Chapter Five in your textbook, you might end class by asking students to answer one of the prediction questions at the beginning of Chapter Six. When they are sitting down to read Chapter Six that evening or the next day, and spot that question again, they will recall the predictions they made in class, which should (re)-activate their prior knowledge.

You can push this activity one step further by asking students to revisit a closing prediction question in the opening minutes of the next class and reflect on whether or not they got it right and why they did (or didn't). To continue with the example from the previous section, let's assume I had presented the three experiments on prediction and learning in my class period on Monday. But I had reserved a fourth case, one that introduces a new wrinkle to the research, for the end of class. In the closing minutes of the period I describe the setup of this last experiment and ask them to predict the results. But this time I send them away without revealing what happened, and leave them with a teaser: "You'll find the results of this experiment in your reading for Wednesday's class." When students return on Wednesday, I can ask a few students to remind me what they had predicted on Monday, to describe the results they read about, and to account for the difference: What principle or new idea explains the discrepancy between the first three experiments and the fourth one?

PRINCIPLES

Asking students to make predictions requires a very small investment of time, which makes predicting an ideal small teaching activity. The following principles can help guide the creation of prediction activities in your classroom.

Stay Conceptual. Remember that part of the reason predictions work is that they require students to draw up whatever knowledge they might have that will assist them in making their prediction. If you ask them questions that are so specific that they have no prior knowledge to activate, you won't see this benefit. It seems unlikely, for example, that asking students to predict the meaning of a word in a language with which they are totally unfamiliar, in a different alphabet, will offer much learning benefit. Focus prediction activities on the major conceptual material that will maximize their learning in the course.

Provide Fast Feedback. Close the loop on every prediction your students make by providing feedback as immediately as possible. Predictions made at the opening of a class session should be addressed within that class session. Those made at the end, even if they will be answered by the reading or studying that they will do for the next session, should still be reviewed at the opening of that next session. Predictions made in online environments should provide feedback within the same session they are made. Remember that you don't want wrong predictions hanging around in students' heads for very long; the more immediate the correction, the better.

Induce Reflection. As Daniel Willingham has argued, "Memory is the residue of thought" (Willingham 2014, p. 54). In other words, we remember what we spend a little time thinking about. Prediction provides an excellent spur for thought, in that you can ask students to think about why they made their prediction, what actually happened (if the prediction leads to direct observation), and why their prediction was right or wrong. If you are asking students at the beginning of a class to write down a prediction and having a few of them read their predictions aloud, return to those students at the end of class and ask them to explain why they made those predictions. Students who made correct predictions can be asked to articulate the principle or concept that helped them get it right; students who made incorrect predictions can repair their understanding by articulating the correct ideas.

SMALL TEACHING QUICK TIPS: PREDICTING

Predictive activities are the ideal starting point for a small teaching approach, because they are so easy to slot into the opening and closing of a learning unit. These reliable prediction activities give you some practical starting points.

- Open the course with a class brainstorming activity in which you ask students to surface their prior knowledge. Give them time individually or in small groups, and then work as a class to organize that knowledge in ways that will set up the learning to come.
- At the beginning of the class, unit, or course, give students a brief pretest on the material. For example, give an opening-week pretest that is similar in format to the final exam.
- Use classroom polling to break up your course lectures and ask students questions about the next topic you will cover. Pose the question, have them respond with whatever poll technology you are using, and then invite some paired or whole-class discussion of their responses before you move into your explanation.
- When presenting cases, problems, examples, or histories, stop before the conclusion and ask students to predict the outcome. Invite them to reflect afterward on why they got it wrong or right. In other words: pause, predict, ponder.
- Close class by asking students to make predictions about material that will be covered in the next class session.

CONCLUSION

As I was finishing the second edition of this book, an article appeared in a psychology journal which provided another plank of support for the power of prediction, as well as one more reason why prediction has such a positive impact (Brod 2021). The article describes an experiment in which the researchers asked students to predict the scores of a soccer game, then revealed the correct scores to them, and afterward tested their memory of those scores. But they compared the students who engaged in these predictive activities to another group of students who did something slightly different: they were shown the correct scores, and then asked to explain whether those scores matched their expectations about them. In other words, the students in that second group were essentially being asked: If you *had* made a prediction, would it have been correct? As you might expect from the research I have provided throughout this chapter, the students who made the actual predictions had better memory for the soccer games than did the students who only reflected afterward upon how well the scores matched their expectations. The concrete act of making the prediction was the crucial differentiator: they had to use their prior knowledge of soccer to hazard a prediction, and then see the results afterward.

The researchers in this study added one interesting element to their experiment, though. They looked at the pupil dilation of the subjects as the answer was revealed to them. When the subjects who had made predictions saw the correct answers, their pupils dilated, indicating surprise. The researchers thus argue that one of the driving mechanisms behind the learning power of prediction is the quick emotional burst we get from seeing how our prediction turns out. As we shall discuss further in Chapter Eight, emotions can play a key role in enhancing our learning. In this experiment, the predictions that the subjects made about the soccer games heightened their emotional investment in finding out the scores, and this emotional investment paid dividends in their learning. This finding on the emotional impact of prediction led the researchers to conclude that random guessing doesn't have the same impact as prediction. When I make a random guess, I'm aware of its randomness, and don't make an emotional commitment to it. When I make a prediction, I'm drawing on my prior knowledge to try to understand a novel situation, and as a result I become more emotionally invested in the outcome: I want to know if I was right. It's that emotional investment, the researchers argue, that makes the difference, and that helps lodge the new knowledge firmly in my brain.

Keep this finding in mind as you are engineering predictive activities for your students. If you give them a pretest, encourage them to draw on their previous knowledge to try and get as many correct as possible. If you are asking students to predict something in class with electronic polling, actually give them the time they would need to think about it and make that prediction. The more they commit themselves to their predictions, the more emotion they will feel at the revelation of the correct answer—and the more they are likely to remember it in the future.

Chapter 2

Retrieving

INTRODUCTION

I wrote almost every word of the first edition of this book sitting in a coffee shop about two blocks from my home. Most weekdays I would walk in, find a spot near an electrical outlet, fire up my laptop, and then head to the counter to order my beverage. I am a person of routines when it comes to food and drink, so every day for about six months I placed the same order: medium green tea. The coffee shop had its routines as well, which meant that most of the time I was placing my order with the same young woman. Yet, in spite of the fact that she saw my smiling face three or four days a week making the same order, she always looked up at me expectantly when I arrived, as if I had not requested the same thing a hundred times before. She would even ask me the same two questions about my tea order every time: "Hot or cold?" "Honey or lemon?" Hot and No. Every time. As the weeks and months of this stretched on, it became a mild source of amusement to me to see if she would ever remember my order. She never did. Until, that is, I walked in one day and felt a little mischievous.

"Can I help you?" she said.

"Can you guess?" I replied.

She looked up as if seeing me for the first time, and she smiled sheepishly.

"Oh gosh," she said. "Why am I blanking?"

"It's OK," I said. "No problem. Medium green tea. Hot, nothing in it."

The next time I showed up at the coffee shop was a couple of days later. I walked in, found my spot, fired up the laptop, and approached my forgetful friend at the counter. To my astonishment, she pointed at me with a smile and said:

"Medium green tea, hot, no honey or lemon?"

This little story illustrates perfectly a learning phenomenon called the retrieval effect (and sometimes also called the testing effect). Put as simply as possible, the retrieval effect means that if you want to retrieve knowledge from your memory, you have to *practice* retrieving knowledge from your memory. The more times that you practice remembering something, the more capable you become of remembering that thing in the future. Every time I walked into that coffee shop and told the barista my order, she was passively receiving that information from me; she did not have to draw it from her memory. She was doing the student equivalent of staring at her notes over and over again—a practice that cognitive psychologists will tell you is just about the most ineffective study strategy students can undertake (Weinstein and Sumeracki 2019, pp. 23–25). When I made one very small change to our interaction by "testing" her to remember my order—even though she didn't get it right—she had to practice, for the first time, drawing that piece of information from her memory. And because it was such a simple piece of information, one practice was enough to help her remember it for the next time. It won't be quite as simple for our students, who have to remember more complex stuff than my order at the coffee shop. But the principle is exactly the same. The more times any of us practice remembering something we are trying to learn, the more firmly we lodge it in our memories for the long term.

The retrieval effect is also sometimes called the testing effect as a way to help teachers recognize its significance for student learning in their classrooms. Teachers (and students and parents) typically think about tests as a means to measure student learning. But tests, thought about in the most general way possible, are actually memory exercises. And if the research suggests that memory exercises improve our memories, that should mean that tests have the potential not just to measure learning but also actually to improve it. The problem with using the phrase *the testing effect* is that many of us have a very limited understanding of what the word *test* means—it recalls for us anxious students biting their pencil erasers as they sweat their way through a multiple-choice final exam. But, of course, testing can happen in a thousand different ways, from small daily quizzing exercises to oral examinations to online short-answer questions. The research that we will consider in this chapter encompasses multiple types of these testing activities, all of which help students exercise their memory muscles to improve and solidify their knowledge base. Testing, here, simply means forcing learners to recall learned information, concepts, or skills from their memory. It can take the form of oral questioning in the first five minutes of class just as easily as it can take the form of a high-stakes final exam. For that reason, I will continue to speak primarily of the retrieval effect and retrieval practice in what follows to avoid limiting your thinking about how you might manifest this teaching strategy in your classroom, and especially to help you think about how to implement retrieval practice through a variety of small teaching activities.

IN THEORY

A host of experiments designed to illustrate the power of the retrieval effect have come from the Memory Lab of Henry L. Roediger at Washington University in St. Louis, which houses multiple researchers exploring the educational implications of their work on learning, cognition, and memory. As Roediger and his co-authors report in *Make It Stick: The Science of Successful Learning*, in 2006 researchers from the Memory Lab began working with a middle school in Columbia, Missouri, to see whether they could leverage the power of the retrieval effect in order to improve student learning in real classrooms (Brown, Roediger, and McDaniel 2014). Then-research associate Pooja K. Agarwal worked with a sixth-grade social studies teacher, Patrice Bain, to explore whether a structured set of retrieval practice activities in her six classes would help improve her students' learning. Rather than using retrieval practice with some of the classes and not with others, they divided the course material—standard-issue middle-school social studies textbook stuff, covering major world civilizations—into three groupings and treated each of those groupings differently. For the first set of material, the students were given three opportunities to practice retrieval in the form of regular quizzes, which were spaced out in the following way: one at the beginning of class, after they had read course material for homework, but prior to the teacher discussing it; one at the end of class, after discussion of the material; and one just before each major test for the class. The teacher excused herself from the room during the quizzes; the students were shown the correct answers after they had completed the quizzes, but they did not count toward their grades. For the second grouping of material, students had the opportunity to restudy key concepts from the course that would appear on the exams. Bain covered the third grouping of material with her usual teaching methods, without any additional study or retrieval practice. It's worth noting, before discussing the results, that the additional retrieval practice used with the first grouping of material did not come *in addition to* students' normal classroom time. It took place within the regular classroom hours, which means it was substituting for something else—lectures, class discussions, independent study time, or whatever else the teacher did on non-quiz days. This deserves notice because some teachers might fear that retrieval practice will take time away from other, more important learning activities.

The experiment yielded, for our purposes, three important results. First and foremost, the authors explain, it demonstrated the potency of retrieval practice: "The kids scored a full grade level higher on the material that had been quizzed than on the material that had not been quizzed" (Brown, Roediger, and McDaniel 2014, p. 35). A year later the research group tried this same experiment in eighth-grade science courses at the same school, and the results were even stronger: "At the end of three semesters, the eighth graders averaged 79 percent (C+) on the science material that had not been quizzed, compared to 92 percent (A-) on the material that had been quizzed" (p. 35). Both of these experiments reveal the incredible power of retrieval practice to improve students' long-term mastery of core knowledge. Course grades on material that was the subject of regular retrieval practice, in the form of standard course quizzing, were at least a full letter higher than course grades on non-quizzed material.

A second important result of the original experiment was that the grades on the second grouping of material (for which the students had been given additional study time) were no better than the grades on the third grouping of the material (which had no special intervention at all). In other words, additional study time provided them with no additional learning benefit. "Mere re-reading," the authors conclude, "does not much help" (p. 35). Finally, and perhaps most importantly, the positive results of the experiment extended far out in time: "The testing effect persisted eight months later at the end-of-year exams" (p. 35). This has obvious implications for us as teachers; we want students to remember our course material beyond the initial testing period, and spaced-out retrieval practice (more on this spacing in Chapter Three) seems to have a powerful impact on long-term learning. But it's worth repeating the main point of these results one last time: a brief (and ungraded) multiple-choice quiz at the beginning and end of class and one additional quiz before the exam raised the grades of the students by a full letter grade.

Let's consider two more demonstrations of the power of retrieval practice, each of which will add some nuance to our understanding of the role it can play in education.. A 2007 experiment by Roediger and Butler helps confirm what many readers might suspect: not all types of testing are equal. In this experiment, Roediger and Butler had students observe three 30-minute lectures on art history, with slideshows, over a 3-day period. At the end of each lecture, students did one of four things: (a) take a short-answer test on the material they had just learned; (b) take a multiple-choice test on the material; (c) restudy some of the key facts from the lecture; or (d) walk out the door with no additional activity (which of course is what happens at the conclusion of most college classes). The students came back 30 days after the last of the three lectures to take a final short-answer test on the material; this time-lapse created what the authors called "a more realistic timescale over which students may retain classroom lecture information prior to a test." In other words, students often learn material in class and are not tested on it until several weeks later; a final test 30 days after the learning period mimicked that longer interval (p. 517). The students who took the short-answer tests directly after the lectures (group a) scored the highest on the final exam, at 47%; the students who took multiple-choice exams (group b) and had additional study time (group c) scored about equally, at 36%; those who had no activity (group d) scored around 20%. These numbers can seem a little disheartening, but keep in mind that in this experiment students had no reason or opportunity to revisit the course material during the 30-day interval between the lectures and the final exam—which, to a certain extent, makes the results of the students who took the short-answer exam really astonishing, since they recalled almost 50% of the material 30 days later with absolutely no re-exposure or study time.

But this study helps us draw out some nuances. First, the students who performed the best were the ones who had to put the most active thought into their answers through short-answer questions. In the pithy formulation of Daniel Willingham, "Memory is the residue of thought" (Willingham 2009, p. 54). Those short-answer questions required students to formulate answers in their own words, and hence to spend more time answering than the multiple-choice questions. Second, note that in this case the students who had the opportunity to engage in what the authors call "focused restudy" did perform better than the students who had no activity at all. So while some experiments have shown little difference between students who had extra study time and students who had no additional study or testing, this one yielded a different, more positive result. Third and finally, the students who scored the highest on the post-30 day test, which was a short-answer test, were the students who had taken previous short-answer tests. This could mean that the similarity in format between the two types of questions produced the better learning results. In other words, it may be that answering multiple-choice questions at the conclusion of a lesson produces one type of learning, and that type of learning does not translate well into performing well on short-answer questions.

To address that possibility, and to make a case for the special power of writing and problem-solving activities as a part of your retrieval practice, I want to consider one final experiment, this one conducted not by memory researchers in the laboratory but by the instructor in a real set of college chemistry courses. Brian Rogerson details in this study the result of an experiment he conducted over five semesters of teaching introductory chemistry at Richard Stockton College in New Jersey. During three of those semesters, which included his first year as a full-time faculty member, he taught using standard lecture techniques. During two of them, he made only one simple change to the course: 10 minutes before the end of each 75-minute class period, he stopped and asked students to respond to a question on the material he had just covered in the lecture. This question was the chemistry equivalent of a short-answer question, as you can see in this example: "Give two reasons that K is more reactive than Li." Some of them required answers in the form of equations or formula, but all of them required more than just repetition from memory. The students wrote their answers down twice—once on a form that they returned to him and once on a paper to keep. This allowed Rogerson to review the answers prior to the next class—though he did not grade or return them—and then to address problems in their responses at the beginning of that next class session, with students able to check the answers they had given.

In the three semesters in which he did not conduct these end-of-class assessments (which he derived from Angelo and Cross's justly famous book *Classroom Assessment Techniques*) the rate of students who failed or withdrew from the course was 35%. In the semesters in which he used the technique, that rate fell to 17%. The number of Cs and Ds rose in the assessment semesters, which means that students who would have dropped were now performing at the C and D levels—not a miraculous transformation, but an impressive one nonetheless. The rates of A and B students stayed roughly stable in both cohorts, which may partially reflect the fact that an A or B student doesn't have as much room to improve as a C or D student does. Interestingly, in his introduction and discussion of this experiment, Rogerson made no mention of the possibility that retrieval practice may help explain the results of this experiment. Like most instructors who use assessments of any kind, he implemented it as a means to gauge the learning of his students and then saw it as an opportunity to provide feedback on their work. But you will note the similarity between the small task he required of his students and what the researchers in our last experiment required of their subjects: directly following the lecture, they asked students short questions about the material they had just covered. The results of such questions can be disheartening, as Rogerson pointed out: "Even after classes in which I felt I had explained something very well and thoroughly, there were students for whom the answer to the assessment was not obvious" (Rogerson 2003, p. 163). But even when students are frequently providing wrong answers, as they did for Rogerson and will do in your classes—and as long as you provide them feedback to help them correct their mistakes—the results of these experiments are hard to dismiss.

It remains for us only to understand why the retrieval effect happens. The very short version is that memory researchers these days seem to believe that our long-term memories are capable of holding a huge amount of material. As cognitive psychologist Michelle Miller writes in *Minds Online*, "There's wide consensus among memory researchers that long-term memory is essentially unlimited" (Miller 2014, p. 94). However, that unlimited storage capacity can be as much of a problem as a long-term memory with smaller storage capacity. In an earlier essay on what college teachers should know about memory, Miller explained that "in long-term memory the limiting factor is not storage capacity, but rather the ability to find what you need when you need it. Long-term memory is rather like having a vast amount of closet space—it is easy to store many items, but it is difficult to retrieve the needed item in a timely fashion" (Miller 2011, p. 119). So the challenge for students, or for any of us, is not jamming facts and information down into our long-term memories but instead drawing those facts and information out when we need them or when they will help us in some way. Every time we extract a piece of information or an experience from our memory, we are strengthening neural pathways that lead from our long-term memory into our working memory, where we can use our memories to think and take actions. The more times we draw it from memory, the more deeply we carve out that pathway, and the more we make that piece of information or experience available to us in the future. So retrieval practice, in the form of either informal remembering of things, such as someone's order for a cup of green tea, or formal testing or quizzing in a school environment, paves the way for our memories to strengthen and improve.

Since the publication of the first edition of this book, cognitive psychologist Pooja K. Agarwal has become one of the leading advocates for retrieval practice in education, through her book *Powerful Teaching: Unleashing the Science of Learning* (co-authored with Patrice Bain) and her website RetrievalPractice.org, where you can find both links to further research and plenty of examples of how to use retrieval practice in education. Agarwal points out one additional reason that retrieval practice works: because it's challenging, and we learn more from challenging tasks than we do from easy ones. You'll remember how that barista struggled for a moment when I asked her about my order, and we've all seen students struggling to answer retrieval questions in class or while they are taking quizzes. Those struggles are an essential part of the process, as Agarwal explains:

> Retrieval practice makes learning effortful and challenging. Because retrieving information requires mental effort, we often think we are doing poorly if we can't remember something. We may feel like progress is slow, but that's when our best learning takes place . . . Struggling to learn—through the act of practicing what you know and recalling information—is much more effective than re-reading, taking notes, or listening to lectures. Slower, effortful retrieval leads to long-term learning. In contrast, fast, easy strategies only lead to short-term learning. (Agarwal 2019)

Reward comes from effort, in learning as in almost anything in life. Inviting our students to engage in the struggle to retrieve something from their memories, though perhaps frustrating at first, will ultimately help them obtain the long-term mastery of knowledge that will ensure success in the classroom and beyond.

MODELS

You don't have to think too hard about how to give your students effective retrieval practice; you just have to do it. The stumbling block for instructors arises less from designing strategies than from worrying about time: how much of their classroom or planning time do they want to devote to helping students remember foundational knowledge? Small teaching can come to the rescue here, as it can help instructors envision how to incorporate retrieval practice into bite-sized moments such as the opening and closing minutes of class and into small exercises in online or blended courses.

Opening Questions

The quickest method for cultivating retrieval practice in class takes the form of asking questions, either orally or in writing, about material that either you or the students have covered already. So instead of walking into class and providing an overview of what happened in the last class period or reminding students about the larger unit in which this particular class session is embedded, ask them to provide you with that information:

- Before we start, can anyone remind me what we talked about in class on Monday? How about what we were working on last week?
- Before I introduce the third major theory we will explore in the course, what have been the two main theories we have discussed thus far?

- We've seen several experiments in this area already this semester. Can someone remind me of the results we observed?

I should note from personal experience that if you have never tried this before, you might be surprised and disappointed at how difficult students will initially find such retrieval exercises. They will stare at you with jaws agape when you ask them about material you covered the day before yesterday—material you spent many hours preparing with care in your office. Take heart and persist. The more you do it, the better they will get it—and the better they get at it, the more deeply they are learning it. If you wish to formalize this type of activity, you could follow the lead of Annie Blazer, a professor of religious studies, who begins each class with a single student providing a 3–5-minute summary of the previous class; each student does this at least once per semester (Blazer 2014, p. 344).

Naturally, the same types of questions will work for material that students have read in advance of the class or for any homework problems they have completed. Again, prior to launching a lecture or course activity for the day, ask students to provide you with the highlights of the reading or work they have completed the night before. Students in my classes engage in brief writing exercises along these lines at the start of almost every class. When I started using these exercises, at the beginning of my teaching career, I knew nothing about the power of retrieval practice for learning. I implemented them for a very different reason: to help spark discussion. I had found that just walking into the room and asking students to engage in discussion of complex issues or questions did not work very well; it worked much more effectively if I posed a question, gave them 5 or 10 minutes to write a response, and *then* opened up the floor for discussion. But I also used them as a form of low-level quizzing, just to ensure that students were reading. Every question requires students to do a little bit of remembering and a little bit of thinking. If students have been assigned the first 75 pages of a novel for a class, for example, I might ask them to describe for me the primary qualities or characteristics of the narrator of the story. The word *primary* requires them to make some judgments about the variety of characteristics they might remember. Over the course of my 20 years of full-time teaching, I have come to recognize that these small writing exercises constitute the best method I have for supporting student learning in my courses—even if, as with most positive teaching experiences I have had, I stumbled upon this strategy through dumb luck or for the wrong reasons. Even though the students groan occasionally about the writing exercises over the course of the (long) semester, they note their value frequently both in conversation with me and in their evaluations of the course.

Brian Rogerson points out in his essay that one of the benefits of asking students to complete questions in writing, as opposed to just orally, is that it demands participation from all students. "These assessments," he writes of his end-of-class questions, "attempt to survey all the students in the class, not just the more vocal ones as occurs when prompting the class for questions" (Rogerson 2003, p. 163). In other words, when you throw out your opening questions orally, you may be concerned that you are providing retrieval practice only for the students who habitually participate in class, thus leaving many other students without this benefit. However, this may not be the case. A memory experiment in which subjects were asked to view a map and to practice retrieval of the map's features *covertly* (i.e., simply by thinking about it and not speaking or writing any answers aloud) still showed boosts to their subsequent ability to reproduce the map from memory. This research suggests that "covert retrieval practice is as good as overt practice in benefitting later retention. . .both methods produce a robust testing effect" (Pyc, Agarwal, and Roediger 2014, p. 80). Of course, this will work only if you provide the opportunity for covert retrieval, which means that you should ask questions, pause for a few moments to allow everyone to engage in retrieval practice, and then invite students to share their responses. Even the students who don't speak the answer aloud can benefit from opening questions if they have a moment to think.

Closing Questions

Extrapolating from opening questions to closing questions doesn't take much creative thinking, and much of the research on retrieval practice—such as the experiment with those art history lectures—has focused on the effects of asking students questions about material they have just learned. So we know that closing questions are an effective small teaching strategy, and the same principles articulated before also apply here: focus on the key concepts that you want students to take away from the class session, and favor writing over oral questions whenever feasible. If you are looking for a simple template for closing questions that will promote retrieval practice (and give you good feedback on the learning of your students), I like the one described by Seth Matthew Fishman and Edward Wahesh in the journal *College Teaching* (Fishman and Wahesh 2020). They call it the Faculty Feedback Form, and it consists of three simple questions that students respond to in writing at the end of class:

- What is one thing I learned from our class readings?
- What is one thing I learned from today's class?
- What am I unclear [about] or would like to know more about?

Fishman and Wahesh have students respond to a fourth question that varies from week to week, and also ask students to provide a rating of their understanding of the week's material from 1 to a 100 every week. This package of activities invites students to retrieve, to think, and to reflect upon the quality of their learning, packing a lot of cognitive punch into a few minutes of class time.

One important point about these first two models is that if you ask students retrieval-based questions either at the beginning or end of the class, you will have to tell them not to look in their notebooks or their textbooks for the answers. I promise you that this will be their first inclination. Throw out a question about what you have just taught them or about what you did in class last week, and they will immediately begin flipping through their notebooks to find the answer. You will have to remind them that you are not conducting a scavenger hunt for answers or a race to see who can find the answer most quickly. You are helping them remember information, and this will benefit them only if they take the time to draw the information from their brains and not their notebooks. If you spend a lot of time reading about experiments in learning and memory, as I have done while preparing and writing both editions of this book, you will notice that almost every experiment uses a control condition in which students simply review their notebooks, textbooks, or key concepts as a study guide. In almost every experiment that I have encountered in this research, *this method proves less effective for long-term retention*. In other words, almost anything that students do with learned information or ideas or skills works more effectively than just looking at your notes about it, even doing so multiple times (Dunlovsky 2013). You might want to explain to your students the purpose of opening and closing questions and how it will help them learn the material more deeply; then they won't be so baffled when you introduce small teaching activities that require them to close their books and notebooks and ask them to remember something they have learned, either at the opening or closing of class.

Online Retrieval

The challenge with implementing retrieval practice in online environments is that students are typically working away from you, so you cannot control whether or not they have access to the materials they are tasked with remembering. So while you might be asking them to remember something, they could be just searching for the answers in their notebooks, which will not give them that valuable retrieval practice. With that said, still consider Miller's (2014) suggestions for small teaching activities or course design tweaks as ways to offer students in online or hybrid courses the opportunity to engage in retrieval practice.

Reading Checks. Retrieval practice can begin when students first engage with course materials that you have put online. Include retrieval type questions at the end of every page or section's worth of material and ensure that students can't get to the next section until they take a brief quiz. This is sometimes referred to as the "conditional release" of material within your learning management system, and is recommended by Flower Darby in *Small Teaching Online* (2019, pp. 35–38). Michelle Miller points to a study in which students who read new material and were quizzed on it in this fashion outperformed nonquizzed students on the final exam. She notes a bonus effect demonstrated by the study: "although the frequent quiz breaks kept students more attentive, they did not seem to tip them over into anxiety; students who did the interspersed quizzes actually reported *less* anxiety about the cumulative test" (p. 78).

Frequent Quizzing. Create or find as large of a question bank as possible and require students to take online quizzes frequently. If the bank is large enough, you can allow multiple retakes of the quiz, which would help boost memory because each retake will constitute another instance of retrieval practice. (If the bank is not large enough, you can run into problems with cheating.) As the experiment with the art history lectures demonstrates, and as Miller notes as well, "Short-answer questions do produce a moderate advantage over multiple choice" (p. 108). However, as she also notes, "The best quiz is the one that students will actually *do*—so don't let the perfect be the enemy of the good as you work to create more frequent testing opportunities" (p. 108). If multiple-choice quizzes will ease your grading burden and give you time to create more questions, use multiple-choice questions. Setting time limits on the quiz can help ensure that students don't have a wide-open window to search around in their course materials for answers and might encourage more of them to engage in true retrieval practice on your quizzes.

Space Out Due Dates. When you are creating the due dates for your online course, space them out so that quizzes and assessments are occurring on a very regular and frequent schedule (a good practice for face-to-face courses as well, by the way). The more frequently that your students have to check in and offer some demonstration of their learning, the more often you are giving them retrieval practice. Miller recommends setting up "a recurring weekly schedule where each kind of work (discussion, quizzing, homework, any higher-stakes assignments such as major exams or papers) is due on a different day" (p. 109). Such a recommendation will help both with retrieval practice and with interleaving, another key tool for learning.

The Retrieving Syllabus

I'll finish with a simple suggestion for the use of the syllabus to promote retrieval practice. One of the benefits that a syllabus can provide to students is helping them see the overview of the course topics and how they fit together. For this reason I advocate filling out the course schedule section of your syllabus with as much detail as possible. Include phrases or even sentences that describe what will happen in the different units of the course so that students can keep the syllabus as a living document that guides them throughout the semester. The notion of a "living syllabus" typically refers to the idea that your course will grow and evolve over the semester, which of course any course should do in response to the needs of its students (Lang 2015). But what I mean here is a little more constrained: the syllabus has continued life because you continue to use it as a learning tool throughout the semester.

Such a living syllabus can serve as an excellent small teaching retrieval tool. Require the students to bring their syllabus to class every day, and occasionally use those precious opening and closing minutes of class for a very simple exercise. Have your students pull out their syllabus, and then point them to a previous day's content and ask them to spend a few minutes writing down what they remember about it. You can do this informally, by having them do so in their notebooks, or you could do it in the form of a writing exercise that you collect. You could even do it orally. Point to the date, give them a minute to think, and then collectively ask the class to remind you about what key concepts or skills they took away from that class period or that course unit. Too often, the course syllabus makes an appearance on the first day of the semester and then remains buried in a folder for the rest of the course, serving only as a list of due dates or assignments to complete. Use your course syllabus as a means to foster retrieval practice through brief, small teaching moments in individual class sessions.

PRINCIPLES

Retrieval practice will help your students retain foundational material, which they are most likely to encounter in introductory or entry-level courses in your field. Hence when you are considering how to incorporate retrieval into your teaching repertoire, look first to the lower-level classes you are teaching. The following principles can help guide you through the use of the models above or through the creation of alternative retrieval exercises tailored to your courses.

Frequency Matters. The first and last implication of all of this research on retrieval practice is very straightforward: the more students practice retrieval, the better they learn. Frequency matters. The easiest way to implement frequent practice is through regular quizzing. That should be your default strategy. Give quizzes at least once a week, and don't hesitate to give them every class. But all of that quizzing can mean lots of grading, especially if you are using short-answer questions. If you don't want to rely exclusively on quizzes, mix quizzing with small teaching questions (either orally or in writing) at the opening or close of class. Whatever strategy or mix of strategies you choose, implement them as frequently as possible given all of the other demands on your time.

Align Practice and Assessments. Whatever type of memory tasks you will ask of your students on your high-stakes assessments (such as midterms and exams) should appear in the retrieval practice you use. If you ask students to remember names and dates of key thinkers in your field on the final exam, make sure they are getting practice in remembering those thinkers throughout the semester. If you give multiple-choice final exams, use polling questions in class to give them practice in multiple-choice retrieval. If you give them essay exams that require some memory mixed in with thinking, give them writing exercises in class in which they have to answer final exam-type questions.

Require Thinking. Remember Willingham's axiom that we remember what we think about? Help your students remember by giving them something to think about. Your retrieval practice might sometimes take the form of simple memory exercises—after all, we likely all have certain key facts or basic information that we want students to have mastered. For example, I want students in my British literature survey course to know that Robert Burns is Scottish because his Scottish identity helped influence much of what he wrote. They can't do higher order analysis of a Burns poem on a final exam if they forget that key fact. But rather than asking students to practice remembering his nationality by selecting it from a list, I can ask them short-answer questions that require them to remember that fact and put it to some use: How does the national identity of Robert Burns influence his writing?

SMALL TEACHING QUICK TIPS: RETRIEVING

Memory retrieval works especially well in brief classroom interventions. You can find room for retrieval in almost any class period or learning session, even if it takes only a minute. But my favorite opportunities for retrieval appear in the opening and closing moments of class, or in the form of regular quizzes or writing exercises.

- Open class periods or online sessions by asking students to remind you of content covered in previous class sessions; allow students time to reflect for a few moments if you do so orally.
- Close class by asking students to write down the most important concept from the homework and the class period and one question or confusion that still remains in their minds.
- Close class by having students take a short quiz or answer written questions about the day's material or solve a problem connected to the day's material.

- Give frequent, low-stakes quizzes (at least weekly) to help your students seal up foundational course content; favor short answers or problem solving whenever possible so that students must process or use what they are retrieving.
- Use your syllabus to redirect students to previous course content through quizzes or oral questions and discussion.

CONCLUSION

I have heard college and university professors express reluctance at the use of regular quizzing because they feel like it infantilizes the students or changes the atmosphere of the classroom from one of shared learning and discussion to one of testing and evaluation. I had those exact same feelings about quizzing when I began my teaching career. I just wanted to engage in interesting discussions with my students about literature and not impede our relationship with heavy-handed tactics like quizzing and testing.

However, I had too many experiences of having interesting discussions about literature with students who had not done the reading (but who were very good at faking their way through discussions) and who remembered nothing of what we had discussed at the end of the semester for that perspective to last very long. So I understand any emotional hesitation you might feel at the prospect of regular retrieval practice in your classroom, but remember that such practice helps your students learn foundational knowledge as effectively as anything else we know. Think about retrieval practice as I have been arguing for it here: as an activity that lends itself perfectly to small teaching and therefore doesn't require you to devote huge amounts of time or energy to it.

If you consider it in that light and push yourself to implement regular quizzing or retrieval practice, you will likely find that your students are grateful for it by the end of the semester. In addition to the memory practice it provides them, it also ensures that they stay on top of the reading or homework, which means they won't find themselves stuck at the end of the semester with lots of catching up to do. As always, you can help them recognize the value of those quizzes by teaching transparently. Tell them what the research says about the value of quizzing and retrieval practice and about your decision to use it. They still might not love taking quizzes during the long slogging weeks of October, but they will recognize their value and reap the rewards on those final assessments in December.

Chapter 3

Interleaving

INTRODUCTION

One of the sabbatical projects I undertook while writing the first edition of this book was learning Spanish, a task I had attempted but then abandoned during graduate school many years ago. Although ostensibly I embarked upon this more recent endeavor in preparation for some upcoming travel to Latin America, in truth I count studying and learning languages as one of my favorite pastimes. (I will pause here to allow you to savor the fact that you probably lead a more socially engaging life than I do.) My school language learning includes Latin, Greek, and French, but I have also made independent efforts to learn Spanish, Italian, and Gaelic at various points in my life. Because I have spent so many hours memorizing foreign language vocabulary and studying grammatical structures of other languages, the process has become one with which I am comfortable and familiar. Even though it had been quite a few years since I launched a full and earnest effort to master a language, I assumed that my Spanish study would come easily enough as long as I put in the requisite time and effort.

My course of study began with an online program that I hoped would guide me through the early stages of review and basic acquisition, after which I would expand to other activities like reading novels or watching television shows in Spanish. For a month or two, I spent 15 minutes every day listening to brief sentences in Spanish, repeating them back into the computer microphone, translating Spanish sentences into English and vice versa, and taking occasional quizzes. The individual lessons of the program were broken into segments that took about five minutes to complete, which meant I could complete three new ones every day. Each new segment included a small measure of reinforcement of the material I had already learned, but the lessons focused mostly on acquiring new vocabulary or identifying new rules of grammar or syntax. A month into following this schedule of three new lessons per day, I found myself increasingly forgetting vocabulary I had learned just days before and regularly failing the occasional timed quizzes. I would learn the word for "tie" (*corbata*), and then the next day mix it up with the word for "belt" (*cinturon*). A few weeks later, one of those words would pop up for review, and I wouldn't remember either of them. My progress in understanding Spanish seemed very slow in contrast to my previous experiences. Every lesson felt like a new struggle to me. I assumed that the program—which multiple people had recommended to me—had been constructed by folks who knew something about language acquisition and that therefore the problem must lie with me. Either I was not spending enough time on my study, or my aging brain was no longer as adept as it once was in learning languages. All I could think to do was redouble my time and effort.

Then one day I noticed a tab on the home page labeled Strengthen Skills. I clicked on it, and it took me through a five-minute review session that mimicked the activities of the normal lessons but introduced nothing new; it was like a remixed return of exercises I had completed in the past. At first, I found it frustrating to complete these exercises since I was stumbling over vocabulary that I had supposedly learned already, but I began gradually incorporating more and more of these review sessions into my learning time. Eventually my routine shifted from three new lessons per day to one new lesson per day and two review sessions. Within weeks of making this change I felt the budding mastery that had been eluding me begin to emerge; I began regularly acing the timed quizzes and feeling much more comfortable with my pronunciation efforts. Of course, my progress through new material slowed down, but this seemed like a small price to pay for a much firmer understanding of the new material through these repeated review sessions. Perhaps most important, what had felt like a painful struggle to me now became enjoyable.

IN THEORY

The learning principle that helps explain this improvement in my language acquisition skills is called interleaving, and it involves two related activities that promote high levels of long-term retention: (a) spacing out learning sessions over time; and (b) mixing up your practice of the skills you are seeking to develop. The learning literature contains bodies of research on both of these practices, which scholars usually distinguish with the terms *spacing* and *interleaving*. I'll follow their lead and use those two different terms in what follows, and the models in this chapter will include recommendations for both spacing and interleaving.

A study conducted almost 30 years ago on French language acquisition in an American high school provides an excellent illustration of the power of spacing (Bloom and Shuell 1981). The researchers divided around 50 students into two groups and charged each group with learning 20 new French vocabulary words in different ways. The first group had a single 30-minute session in which they studied the new vocabulary words and completed three separate tasks on them, such as filling in the French word after receiving the English equivalent. The second group had the exact same length of study time and the exact same set of written exercises, but they were separated into three 10-minute study periods over the course of three consecutive days. The contrast between these two methods is usually described in the literature as *massed* versus *spaced* (or sometimes *distributed*) learning. In massed learning, students complete the study or learning task in a single block of time; in distributed practice, students space out their learning sessions over more than one session. At the end of the study periods for both groups in this experiment, the students were given a vocabulary test on the words; both groups averaged about 16 of 20 words correct. This finding will appear again and again in the literature; for short-term retention, massed practice can be as effective (and sometimes more effective) than distributed practice. The researchers then returned to the classroom a week later, without any prior warning to the students, and tested them on the vocabulary again. This time the results diverged sharply: the massed practice students remembered around 11 of the vocabulary words, whereas the spaced practice students remembered around 15. Remember that both groups had the same total learning time and completed the same tasks; only the spacing of their learning activities differed.

A substantial body of research has demonstrated the power of spaced learning. "The benefit of spaced practice," write Megan Sumeracki and Yana Weinstein in *Understanding How We Learn: A Visual Guide* (with illustrations by Oliver Caviglioli), "is arguably one of the strongest contributions that cognitive psychology has made to education" (2019, p. 99).The theory that explains the power of spaced learning stems at least in part from what we have learned about the importance of retrieval practice. One of the challenges to our memories is the ability to pull desired information from our long-term memories when we need it. The more times we practice drawing specific skills or information from our long-term memory, the better we get at it. When we engage in massed learning, putting all of our study into one time period, we never have to access the learned material from the deeper recesses of our long-term memory. By contrast, if we use spaced learning to allow some time for the forgetting of learned material to set in, we are forced to draw material from our longer-term memory when we return to it. Spacing out learning forces us to engage at least partially in memory retrieval.

That forced cycle of forgetting and retrieving is only half the explanation for the power of spaced learning. As the authors of *Make It Stick* explain, the time that intervenes between spaced learning sessions also allows our minds to better organize and solidify what we are studying:

> Embedding new learning in long-term memory requires a process of consolidation, in which memory traces (the brain's representations of new learning) are strengthened, given meaning, and connected to prior knowledge—a process that unfolds over hours and may take several days. Rapid-fire practice leans on short-term memory. Durable learning, however, requires time for mental rehearsal. . . Hence, spaced practice works better. The increased effort to retrieve the learning after a little forgetting has the effect of retriggering consolidation, further strengthening memory. (Brown, Roediger, and McDaniel 2014, p. 49)

Our brains need time to undertake the processes of encoding, consolidating, and organizing newly learned material, and the gaps between spaced learning sessions allow it that time. If you have ever slogged your way through some difficult learning exercise, left it in frustration, and then—hours or days later—returned to it with a mysteriously firmer grasp of it than you had previously, you have experienced the phenomenon described by the authors of *Make It Stick*. I remember this happening to me time and time again when I played the piano more regularly. I would stand up from a practice session convinced that I would never master some difficult passage and then sit down the next day and find that it had mysteriously become much easier than it was the day before.

The implications of this principle are clear enough for both learners and teachers: we should help students space out their learning both in how we design our courses and in how we encourage them to study. However, we can help our students even further if we coordinate their spaced learning with interleaving, a related approach to helping our students master new skills. Interleaving refers to the strategy of learning and practicing the different components of a skill in mixed order. If I were learning to play golf, for example, or trying to improve my skills at the game, I could spend an entire week working on my driving, another week on hitting iron shots, and a third week on putting. This would be what researchers call blocked practice. Interleaving, by contrast, would have me mix up my practice: a couple of days on each skill in every week. The research on interleaving suggests very clearly that the second option will be more likely to improve my skills in the long term. It's easy to see why in this example. When I am playing an actual game of golf, I don't hit 18 drives or 18 putts in a row. I hit a drive, then an iron (or two or three), and then I putt. Throughout the game I am having to make small adjustments to my swing with each different club I use (since they are all slightly different sizes and shapes). When I block my practice, and hit the same club over and over again, I don't have to make those adjustments. Interleaved practice forces me to learn not only how to hit each type of club, but also how to adapt my swing from shot to shot—which is the really essential skill you need to play the game well.

Studies on the power of interleaving in academic settings confirm this explanation. Consider a frequently cited experiment in which students were tasked with the challenge of learning to solve math problems involving different geometric shapes (Rohrer and Taylor 2007). In this experiment the students all received brief tutorials on how to calculate the volume of four different geometric shapes, including seeing a worked example, and then were asked to solve 16 different problems that required them to use what they had just learned. The tutorials and problem-solving sessions took place on two separate occasions, a week apart. In one group, the Blockers, the students had a tutorial and then solved four problems on it; had a second tutorial and then solved four problems on it; and so on. In the other group, the Mixers, the students received all four tutorials at once and then were given the 16 problems in random order. While the students were working on the problems initially, the Blockers performed better. During the first learning session, for example, the Blockers solved 89 percent of the problems correctly; the Mixers solved only 60 percent of them correctly. One week after the practice sessions were completed, the groups returned to the laboratory and were given a new set of eight problems, in random order, two on each of the four shapes. The difference between the groups is astonishing: the success rate of the Blockers dropped down to 20%, whereas the success rate of the Mixers improved to 63%.

In this experiment, both groups engaged in spaced learning; they had two distinct sessions, separated by a week, and the test was given a week after that. We don't have a comparison group in which, say, students completed 32 problems in one massed session instead of the two separate sessions spaced a week apart, but we can assume from previous research on massed versus spaced learning that both the Blockers and Mixers would have outperformed that group. So, given that both groups engaged in spaced learning, this experiment particularly highlights the benefits of interleaved learning: mixing your study or practice as well as spacing it. The authors of the study present this brief explanation for why they believe the Mixers so definitively outperformed the Blockers: "The superior test performance after mixed practice is, in our view, attributed to the fact that students in this condition were required to know not only *how* to solve each kind of problem but also *which* procedure (i.e., formula) was appropriate for each kind of problem (i.e., solid)" (Rohrer and Taylor 2007, pp. 493–494). In other words, the Mixers had to learn not only how to plug and chug the mathematical equations but also how to identify the *type* of problem they were seeing and to select the formula that would work for that problem. They could not work on autopilot, as a student might do in a class session in which he learns Formula A and then applies it to Problem Type A for an extended period of time, knowing that Formula A will always work for Problem Type A, and every problem he will see in the session will be Problem Type A. Hence, "a significant advantage of interleaving and variation," argue the authors of *Make It Stick*, "is that they help us learn better how to assess context and discriminate between problems, selecting and applying the correct solution from a range of possibilities" (Brown, Roediger, and McDaniel 2014, p. 53). And this is important, as they note, because real-world performance contexts require this skill: in life, as on final exams (and in golf), "problems and opportunities come at us unpredictably, out of sequence. For our learning to have practical value, we must be adept at discerning 'What kind of problem is this?' so we can select and apply an appropriate solution" (p. 53). Blocked learning does not require students to make such choices about which learned skill to apply in which context.

This explanation for the limits of blocked practice and the benefits of interleaving points to a deep and fundamental challenge that all learners face: transferring learning from the original context in which we encounter it into novel or unfamiliar contexts. A great deal of research has been done in this area, and the consensus has been that fundamentally we are not very good at doing this. "Transfer," writes Michelle Miller in *Minds Online*, "is remarkably hard to achieve, a particularly unsettling fact given that it is also such a high-stakes issue; after all, an education that doesn't transfer isn't worth much" (Miller 2014, p. 130). We learn in specific contexts, those concepts become familiar to us, and we have trouble transferring that learning into other contexts. So students who learn a specific writing skill in my composition class never think to apply it to the history paper they are writing; students who master the scientific method in biology don't think to apply it in the psychology course they are taking. Blocked study or practice deepens our association between a learned skill or concept and the specific context in which we learned it; interleaved learning, by contrast, forces us into frequent transfers of information and skills across contexts, which helps us develop the ability to recognize when a learned skill might apply in a new context. The students in the math experiment, when they were taking that final test, were faced with novel problems in random order. The students who had engaged in mixed practice were much more effective than the blockers at rooting around in their memory for the full set of skills they had learned and applying them in this new context. Cultivating the ability of our students to draw from memory and apply learned concepts or skills to new situations is, as Susan Ambrose and her colleagues argued, the "central goal of education" (Ambrose, Bridges, DiPietro, Lovett, Norman 2010, p. 108). Interleaved learning facilitates that goal more effectively than massed learning.

Before we push into the models for interleaving in higher education pedagogy, though, I have to offer one essential clarification. In the initial learning phase, blocked study or practice is not a bad thing—and for some types of learning tasks it might even be a necessary thing. A study by Shana Carpenter and Frank Mueller, two psychologists at Iowa State University, compared the effects of blocked and interleaved practice on students who were learning the pronunciations of French words (Carpenter and Mueller 2013). Over the course of several experiments, they found consistently that the students who had the opportunity to repeat the pronunciation of familiar words over and over again in blocked fashion outperformed those who learned those pronunciations in interleaved fashion. Their survey of the literature also points to one or two experiments in which blocked learners have outperformed interleavers on certain types of tasks (although they acknowledge that the bulk of published studies supports interleaving). The final recommendation they make in their conclusion, though, seems like an eminently sensible one: "Rather than using a schedule that is exclusively blocked or interleaved, it may be more advantageous to start with a blocked schedule and then transition to interleaving" (p. 680). Blocked study or practice, it seems to me, is an appropriate first step for any learning activity. As Benedict Carey put it, "It's not that repetitive [or massed] practice is *bad*. We all need a certain amount of it to become familiar with any new skill or material" (Carey 2014a, p. 157). Indeed, I suspect most of us introduce new material to our students, or learn it ourselves, by blocking the study or practice of it. We have to begin the learning process by spending some concentrated time or effort on the task. The argument I am making here is not to eliminate blocked practice but to use interleaving to require students to return continuously, in different contexts, to material they have learned already. Blocking on its own is not a problem; blocking without interleaving—otherwise known as cramming—produces wonderful short-term retention but will leave our students without the long-term retention that will enable them to extend their learning beyond the final exam.

I should conclude by noting that interleaved practice can seem messy and might even provoke frustration from you and your students since it would be much neater and cleaner to march your way through the learning of new skills in order, mastering them completely before moving onto the next. Indeed it would, and the research on both spacing and interleaving confirms what you suspect: learners often find it frustrating. I experienced this frustration myself when I began using that Strengthen Skills tab in my language-learning program and found that I didn't know nearly as much as I thought I did. Research also tells us that massed practice works very effectively for short-term learning, which is why students like it and why they can often perform well on exams when they engage in massed learning exercises like cramming. As long as they are cramming immediately prior to the exam, they will see some benefit from their exertions (Sumeracki, Weinstein, and Caliglioli 2019, pp. 90–92). But if they want their learning to last beyond the next few hours or the next day, they have to take a different approach.

MODELS

The application of the small teaching philosophy to the learning principle of interleaving occurs less in the form of specific in-class activities than in the form of tweaks or modifications to your course design. So the following models focus less on discipline-based examples and more on how to achieve interleaving in three different contexts: (a) through the design of your assessment plan, especially exams and quizzes; (b) through the organization of your class time; and (c) through the use of an online course management system.

Cumulative Exams

If you combine the research on the importance of retrieval practice and the power of interleaving, the implication is an obvious one: all major exams in your course should be cumulative. Research on learning supports this implication. In one study of cumulative versus noncumulative exams in psychology courses, researchers analyzed the scores of students in a cluster of psychology courses on a postcourse assessment; students who had taken a cumulative final exam scored substantially higher on the postcourse assessment than those who had taken noncumulative finals (Khanna, Brack, and Finken 2013). For some of the courses, the positive learning effects of the cumulative final exam persisted as long as 18 months after the completion of the course.

More generally, every major assignment should require students to draw—at least a little bit—on information or concepts or skills they have learned in previous units. This does not have to mean that the third exam of the course must be divided into three parts, one on each of the first three units. It may be that the third exam focuses primarily on the third unit, with two-thirds or three-quarters of the tested material deriving from that section of the course. But the final third or quarter should require students to return to material from earlier parts of the course. You can even accomplish this in a less obvious way by giving assignments or asking exam questions that require students to compare current content or skills with previously learned material. In my literature survey course, which divides into four units over the course of the semester, each exam requires students to answer three or four large essay questions. After the first exam, one of those questions always requires them to compare an author or event or trend from the current period with one from a previous period. They are warned about this, which gives me an opportunity to remind them about the importance of continually returning to the authors and ideas we have already discussed.

Cumulative Quizzes

Quizzes represent another excellent opportunity to leverage the power of spacing and interleaving in your courses. Select some reasonable percentage of your quizzes that will be devoted to previously covered material and stick with it throughout the semester. If you give 10-question multiple-choice quizzes on a weekly basis, set aside two questions for previously learned material. If you give one-question writing-based quizzes, as I do, ensure that every third or fourth quiz requires students to return to previously learned material. In *Powerful Teaching*, Patrice Bain describes her use of what she calls "Big Basket Quizzes," which occur at the end of every week (Agarwal and Bain 2019, pp. 98–99). The basket contains the quiz questions that she has asked all throughout the course. Each end-of-week quiz includes questions focused on the material from the current week as well as some questions pulled from the big basket. This process randomizes the material that students will return to each week, which you might find easier to implement than overthinking the process and creating some kind of algorithm for how and when previous questions appear again. As the course progresses throughout the year, Bain culls from the basket questions which are focused on less essential course content, thus ensuring that the questions students encounter from previous units are the most important ones to be able to answer.

Overall, you should consider your total package of quizzes and exams as the ideal tool for continuously reinforcing learned material from the first week of the semester to the last. If you don't give a cumulative final exam, you are essentially conveying to students that what they learned in the first weeks of the semester don't matter anymore. If you do give a cumulative final exam but not cumulative mid-terms or quizzes that test them on previously learned material, you are not giving them the kind of help they really need to solidify and enhance their early-semester learning on the cumulative exams.

I would be omitting a truth you would quickly discover on your own if I did not reiterate at this point that students might not respond with unbridled enthusiasm (at least initially) to either cumulative exams or cumulative quizzes. Just as I felt frustration when I first began to test myself on previously learned Spanish vocabulary and quickly realized how little of it I remembered, your students might feel initial frustration at the expectation that everything they have learned remains on the table for all of their quizzes and exams. Maryellen Weimer, in a post on cumulative exams on the website Faculty Focus (Weimer 2015), offers some excellent suggestions for helping reconcile students to cumulative exams, all of which sit perfectly within the framework of small teaching activities, requiring just a small investment of class time:

- Open each class session by posting a test question from a previous exam or a potential test question related to previous course content. Give students time to consider and discuss their answers.
- Close class sessions by asking students to create a test question based on that day's material, and pose that question back to them in future class sessions.
- Open or close class sessions by asking students to open their notebooks to a previous day's class session and underline the three most important principles from that day; allow a few moments for a brief discussion of what they featured from their notes.

Strategies like these give you the opportunity to announce to students from the beginning of the semester that all learning in the course will be cumulative, and they give your students the help they need in preparing to succeed on cumulative exams.

Mixing Classroom Practice

In Chapter Five I will make the case that you should give students time in the classroom to practice whatever kinds of skills they will need to complete for your assessments. If you are giving cumulative exams and mixing up skills and knowledge in your quizzes, you need to provide opportunities for students to practice these activities in class. Your final assessment will almost certainly not provide students with an explanation for what skills or knowledge they need to apply on every question of the exam, or on every page of the paper. It will require them to discriminate and adapt, to understand how to take the many skills they have learned in your course and apply them in novel contexts. Your students should get some practice at doing these things in class. To accomplish this, you'll have to consider how you can make practice sessions in your classroom opportunities for spacing and interleaving. If you teach writing, you probably have students write in class; what would spacing and interleaving look like there? If you teach math, you have students solving problems in class sometimes; what would spacing and interleaving look like there? This can be a challenging question to answer, but it's worth at least a little reflection.

Every year or two I teach Introduction to Literature, a course in which we help students learn to interpret literature by marching them through lots of reading in three major genres: poetry, fiction, and drama. Almost every literature textbook on the market, and almost every syllabus I have seen for this kind of course, has students learning how to interpret these three genres in blocked ways. We spend five weeks working on poetry, studying things like symbolism and imagery; five weeks working on fiction, studying things like character and setting; and five weeks on drama, studying things like irony and performance. This obscures the fact that almost any of the interpretive tools they are learning can be applied to any of the three genres. Symbols appear in poems, but they appear in stories and plays as well. Plays have characters, but so do stories and even poems, in the form of the speaker. In my introductory literature course, students spend plenty of time working individually or in groups engaging in interpretive practice: I might put them in groups and ask each group to identify all of the images and potential symbols they can find in a poem, or to analyze a story through the lens of setting and character. If I want them to interleave, at least every once in a while I need to give them a work of literature, along with a list of every interpretive strategy we have studied in class (from all three genres), and say: you tell me which strategies we should use here, and don't limit yourself to the ones we discussed in relation to that genre. In fact, to really drive home the point, I might require them to select at least one interpretive strategy that we *didn't* consider when we were learning that genre. This will force them to consider which strategies to apply in a novel context, and how to do so—which are the core skills that interleaving should help people master.

Consider what the equivalent of this would be in your course. What would it look like to set aside 15 minutes of class time every week or every other week, give students a novel problem or question and a list of everything they have learned thus far, and say: How will you solve it? The more of this work that your students do, the more successful they will be when they get to the novel context of your final assessment—and the novel contexts they will encounter beyond your course.

Online Learning Environments

In *Minds Online*, Michelle Miller argues that online learning environments provide an ideal tool for creating spaced and interleaved learning experiences for our students. In a fully online course, she suggests that instructors "set up a recurring weekly schedule where each kind of work (discussion, quizzing, homework, any higher-stakes assignments such as major exams or papers) is due on a different day. You can set things up so that students are welcome to work ahead, but can't fall behind; some will manage to mass their work anyway by turning everything in extremely early, but those students are exceedingly rare" (Miller 2014, p. 109). For the majority of our students the use of such staggered deadlines will have the desired effect, especially if material from different weeks or units regularly appears in the various assessments. Miller also notes that "when you prioritize spacing and interleaving in your course design, you create a much more complex set of deadlines for students" (p. 110), which may lead to hardships for students who sought out the online learning environment because they needed a more flexible learning schedule. Here, as in many areas of teaching, you may not be able to distribute deadlines quite as much as the literature on interleaving would recommend. Even a small bit of attention to the distribution of deadlines and spacing of material should help.

For blended courses, you might think about how the class and online components can work jointly to combine blocked and interleaved learning. Perhaps when you are in the room with students you concentrate on exposure to new content, blocking that material into your 50- or 75-minute face-to-face sessions. Especially if you meet the students only once per week in person, you might find you need to use that space for blocked learning to give them enough initial mastery and confidence to tackle the online work. In the online assignments and discussion boards, by contrast, you could continually push students back to older material or ask them to draw connections between the material covered in the most recent class and previously covered material. You can just as easily reverse this strategy, giving online assignments in ways that will focus their attention on specific skills and using your face-to-face time to require them to mix practice and pull skills and ideas from throughout the course. Neither approach seems inherently better to me; it likely depends on the type of material you are teaching. However, it seems to me like a natural fit to make deliberate use of face-to-face and online course components to support both blocked and interleaved learning, whether you are doing so in a fully blended course or even in a traditional face-to-face course that uses any of the features of a learning management system, including quizzes or discussion boards. All these recommendations represent small design shifts that can be addressed as you are laying out the basic plan for your course.

PRINCIPLES

Remember that you can use both spaced learning and interleaving to boost long-term retention. The smallest teaching step would be to find simple ways to space out student exposure to key course material through cumulative quizzes and exams. If you see positive results, you can then work more gradually on designing an assessment system that creates more fully interleaved learning.

Block and Interleave. Blocked learning sessions probably form the backbone of the course plan for many instructors, including me. The research cited in this chapter does not require you to subtract blocked learning sessions from your course; it recommends that you add spacing and interleaving to them. To gain some initial mastery of new content or a novel skill, learners may well need some initial sessions of blocked or massed practice, as the experiment with students learning French pronunciation would suggest (Carpenter and Mueller 2013). Don't hesitate to dig into a focused problem-solving session or to spend concentrated periods of time introducing new content. Just ensure that students return to that material over and over again throughout the semester, encountering it in multiple contexts so that they can continually develop and refine their knowledge and skills.

Keep It Small, Keep It Frequent. As with retrieval practice, frequency matters when it comes to interleaving. Students should have the opportunity to return to key course concepts or skills multiple times over the course of the semester, both in class and on their assessments. If you provide at least one opportunity for interleaving in every week or class unit, and on every quiz or exam, you should be able to cycle back to major elements of the course several times. To help you accomplish this task, keep your interleaving sessions in class small. As with prediction and retrieval, you can use the opening and closing minutes of class to link students to previous course content or even to point them toward future content. Use those windows to pose and discuss previous test or assignment questions, have them solve an additional problem, or highlight and review older material.

Explain and Support. Learning through interleaving can seem frustrating to learners, at least initially. In experiments in which learners have the opportunity to learn through blocked or interleaved practice, they overwhelmingly choose blocked practice because it gives them a feeling of mastery over the material. Pausing before you have fully mastered something can feel frustrating, as can be the demand to recall material or practice skills you thought you had mastered but then realize you don't know as well as you had imagined. Make sure that you speak to your students about the benefits of interleaving, about the nature of your assessments, and about the differences between short- and long-term learning. Since you might find that initially student grades on cumulative exams are lower, consider giving less weight in the overall course grade to early exams, allowing the students an exam or two to accustom themselves to the challenging nature of interleaved learning.

SMALL TEACHING QUICK TIPS: INTERLEAVING

We can once again look to those fertile opening and closing minutes of the class period for interleaving techniques. But every one of your assessments, from quizzes to papers and tests and presentations, can become a potent tool in your interleaving arsenal.

- Reserve a small part of your major exams (and even the minor ones, such as quizzes) for questions or problems that require students to draw on older course content.
- Use quiz and exam questions that require students to connect new material to older material or to revise their understanding of previous content in light of newly learned material.
- Open or close each class session with small opportunities for students to retrieve older knowledge, to practice skills developed earlier in the course, or to apply old knowledge or skills to new contexts.
- In blended or online courses, stagger deadlines and quiz dates to ensure that students benefit from the power of spaced learning. In blended courses mix the work you do in the different modalities: first exposure in the classroom and review online or vice versa.

CONCLUSION

A reminder about the process by which we grow and evolve as teachers might be the most convincing proof I can offer on the power of spacing and interleaving. If you were to take just one of the models that I have presented in these first three chapters, and try to incorporate it into all of your courses on a weekly basis, you will of course get better at it over time. You'll have a much stronger understanding of how to use the technique effectively in six months than you do the first time you try it. Your improvement will stem in part from the fact that spacing and interleaving are supporting your growing mastery. If you put a small teaching technique on a weekly schedule, you will return to it after time has elapsed in each new week, and then for at least one longer interval of a summer or winter break. During that time away from the teaching, your brain will be working behind the scenes, consolidating your knowledge of the technique, and devising new ways to try it. Each time you step into the classroom with the intention to use it, you'll have to retrieve knowledge from your previous attempts, remembering what worked and what didn't work, and correcting your technique. A little bit of prediction, retrieval, and spacing will all be at work in this process.

But if you commit to trying a new technique in all of your courses—in my case, I might be trying it in my English composition course and my British literature survey course—than you are going to be practicing it in multiple contexts, alternating back and forth between them, just as the research on interleaving would recommend. That movement between the different courses will help you learn to discriminate and fine-tune your understanding. At first, you will try the technique in the same way with all of your courses. Eventually you will start to recognize that each course requires its own nuances of application: In my composition course I might do it this way; in my literature classes I might do it another way. You might come to realize that a particular technique works really well just as I have described it for your first-year students; for your seniors or graduate students you have to do things a little bit differently. You might find that some techniques work really well in some contexts or not in others—a realization that will push you further in your thinking about teaching and open up new insights for the future.

In the closing years of the nineteenth century, William James gave a series of presentations in different venues in which he presented some ideas for how teachers could benefit from discoveries in the budding discipline of psychology. In the book that he later wrote based on those talks, published more than a century ago, he notes the importance of spacing and interleaving for deep learning:

> You now see why 'cramming' must be so poor a mode of study. Cramming seeks to stamp things in by intense application immediately before the ordeal. But a thing thus learned can form but few associations. On the other hand, the same thing recurring on different days, in different contexts, read, recited on, referred to again and again, related to other things and reviewed, gets well wrought into the mental structure. (James, 1900, p. 129)

The English professor in me loves this quote so much for the elegance of that final phrase: "well wrought into the mental structure." If that's the kind of learning you seek for your students, find ways to help them space and interleave.

Part II

Understanding

I devoted the introduction to Part One to convincing you that spending class time helping students acquire knowledge was time well spent—that we can't offload this crucial task to Google™ or expect previous courses to have taken care of that fundamental work. I probably don't need to kick off Part Two by convincing you of the value of helping students to develop understanding, to improve their problem-solving skills, and to become more effective writers or presenters. You probably conceive of your role as a teacher primarily in terms of doing that work, as indeed you should. If you are reading this book—or any book like this one—you are also likely already a practitioner of teaching strategies that foster what we might label active learning, in which students spend at least some time *doing* things in the classroom rather than merely sitting there passively. However, the literature that you will see cited in the next three chapters suggests that to assist students in developing their comprehension or acquiring complex cognitive skills such as solving math problems or interpreting a poem, we have to do more than invite questions, hold discussions, use group work, or assign online drill work. We may certainly want to do some or all of these things—but if we do them, we must do them deliberately, with eyes wide open, and with the help of the literature on human learning. Too often, instructors assume that teaching by discussion (or group work or. . .) rather than lecturing will automatically translate into active learning, and deeper understanding. Unfortunately, this is not always the case.

The current term that springs to mind when college and university teachers think about active learning is the *flipped classroom*, which has become a catch-all phrase used to describe classroom structures in which students gain first exposure to course content outside of the classroom and then spend their time within the classroom doing things like solving problems, thinking critically, and writing. This structure—which has been standard operating procedure in many humanities classrooms for decades now—flips the traditional model of higher education in science, technology, engineering, and mathematics (STEM) disciplines, in which instructors provided first exposure through lectures in the classroom and then sent students off to *do* things outside of class. The explosion of new teaching technologies in recent years has enabled more and more instructors to flip their classrooms in this manner and has led to the rapid spread of flipped classrooms in American higher education—not to mention the rapid spread of positive publicity. A press release from a company that promotes learning resources designed for flipped classrooms reported triumphantly in 2013 that around half of all college and university teachers either have tried the flipped classroom or are planning to do so in the near future. Further, "among those employing it already, 57% of faculty agrees that their flipped classroom is 'extremely successful' or 'successful'" (Sonic Foundry 2013). This could strike us as a positive development, given that the majority of instructors are having a positive experience with bringing active learning strategies into their classrooms. But even without being a math professor, I can note that this survey result means that 43% of instructors using a flipped classroom approach are seeing either no improvement in learning or even reduced learning from their gymnastic (and often work-intensive and time-consuming) restructuring of their classrooms.

Robert Talbert, a mathematician and regular contributor to the *Chronicle of Higher Education* who writes frequently about flipped classrooms, notes correctly that opening up the classroom to cognitive activities (rather than simply lecturing and presenting information) represents nothing more than a framing strategy that can have very mixed results:

> The flipped classroom does not automatically provide. . . outstanding learning experiences. What it provides is *space* and *time* for instructors to design learning activities and then carry them out, by relocating the transfer of information to outside the classroom. But then the instructor has the responsibility of using that space and time effectively. And sometimes that doesn't work. [Italics in original] (Talbert 2014)

Careful and strategic design, in other words, matters in the flipped classroom as much as it matters in every other type of classroom, from a large class lecture to a small seminar discussion. I have been teaching the literature professor's version of the flipped classroom since the start of my career now; students read literary texts before class and then come to class and we talk about how to interpret them. But I have walked away from far too many of these discussions, even lively and interesting ones, wondering whether anyone *learned* anything—and especially, whether anyone had acquired something looking like a skill that would help them write their papers or take their exams more effectively.

This applies in the flipped classroom: just because students are busily working away at tasks at their desks doesn't mean they are learning anything.

I still remember a Renaissance literature course I took as an undergraduate in which the instructor put us in small groups with instructions to discuss key passages of whatever text we were studying that day. I loathed those sessions, saw them as pointless, and can assure you I learned nothing from them. Looking back now, through the lens of many years of teaching and reading about teaching and learning in higher education, I can see multiple problems with the way those sessions worked: we had no real task to complete, beyond the vague injunction to discuss the passages; the teacher offered no guidance or supervision while we worked and instead did something inscrutable up at the front of the room; and although a connection may have existed, she did not articulate for us any connection between what we were doing in those group sessions and what we did on our essays or exams. In his introduction to college teaching, *The Missing Course: Everything They Never Taught You About College Teaching*, David Gooblar points out to new teachers that "active learning strategies in and of themselves are not a magic bullet. You can't just use the strategies; you have to know how to use them well" (Gooblar 2019, p. 19). The same holds true for us all. Certain kinds of interactions and feedback are more likely to promote learning than others, just as certain kinds of cognitive activities are more likely to promote learning than others.

The three chapters in this section offer small teaching strategies that should help you design active learning moments in your classroom—whether you think about those moments as flipping or not—in ways that are brief, powerful, and supported by the research on human learning. Any one of the strategies you'll find in these three chapters could become the basis for a full- or even multi-class activity, and the strategies often do serve that function in my own classroom. However, I have tried in the Models section of each chapter to provide examples and ideas for how they could fit into the framework of small teaching. Some of them describe how to conclude a class session with a 10- or 15-minute small teaching activity, and you might think about those activities as the most appropriate ways to conclude a lecture or discussion. But the three major concepts in this part of the book—connecting, practicing, and explaining—could also serve as key design principles for a flipped class session, for effective group work interactions, or for creating new homework assignments or assessments.

The small teaching approaches described in Part One all centered on helping students gain a strong knowledge foundation through effective first exposure and then carefully planned sequencing, repetition, and retrieval. Building learning, though, doesn't quite work like building a house, as we saw in our chapter on interleaving. You don't need or even want to completely master one cognitive activity before moving to the next one. Similarly, as students are developing their knowledge base, they should also be exploring and testing methods to use that knowledge for a wider range of cognitive activities. The following chapters will give you a set of small teaching tools for creating classroom or online experiences that deepen student understanding, improve the ability of your students to analyze and improve their own learning, and become mindful practitioners of a range of cognitive skills.

Chapter 4

Connecting

INTRODUCTION

Although you probably know him primarily as the author of *Animal Farm* and *1984*, British writer George Orwell produced a massive amount of fiction and nonfiction in his lifetime; his complete body of published and unpublished writing totals more than 8,000 pages. Since my disciplinary research in British literature focuses partly on Orwell's work, I've read much (though not quite all) of Orwell's writings, including *A Clergyman's Daughter*, a novel that was little read when it was published and perhaps even less read now. I count it as one of my favorite of Orwell's works, though he had a different opinion of it; he disliked it so much that he forbade it to be republished during his lifetime, after the original printing. The novel's protagonist is Dorothy Hare, the daughter of a selfish and indifferent rector living in the English countryside in the early part of the twentieth century. Dorothy undergoes a traumatic incident in the first half of the novel that results in her waking up in London with total amnesia. After bouts of homelessness and seasonal farm work, she finally winds up as a teacher in a small private school outside of the city. When she first encounters her new pupils, who range in age from 5 or 6 to their late teens, she concludes with despair that the mechanical and rote methods of instruction of their previous teachers have been spectacularly ineffective. Whatever knowledge the students have consists of "small disconnected islets" (Orwell 1986, p. 209) in a vast sea of ignorance. Those scattered bits don't add up to much, Dorothy realizes: "It was obvious that whatever they knew they had learned in an entirely mechanical manner, and they could only gape in a sort of dull bewilderment when asked to think for themselves" (p. 209).

I don't find my students gaping at me too often in dull bewilderment. But Orwell's description of Dorothy's students—one that likely stemmed from the several years he spent teaching at an English boarding school—caught my attention when I first read it because it does capture an experience I have encountered in the classroom more times than I would care to count. It typically happens when I begin pressing students to make connections between disparate sets of concepts or skills in a course—asking them, in other words, to build bridges between the disconnected islets described by Orwell. For example, when we are tackling a new author in my British literature survey course, I might begin class by pointing out some salient feature of the author's life or work and asking students to tell me the name of a previous author (whose work we have read) who shares that same feature. "This is a Scottish author," I will say. "And who was the last Scottish author we read?" Blank stares. Perhaps just a bit of gaping bewilderment. Instead of seeing the broad sweep of British literary history, with its many plots, subplots, and characters, my students see Author A and then Author B and then Author C and so on. They can analyze and remember the main works and features of each author, but they run into trouble when asked to forge connections among writers.

That problem is especially acute at the beginning of a semester. In *How Learning Works*, Susan Ambrose and her co-authors offer a clear explanation for that by noting the different ways novices and experts in a field process and position new knowledge.

Experts, they explain, have a much richer "density of connections among the concepts, facts, and skills they know" (Ambrose, Bridges, DiPietro, Lovett, and Norman 2010, p. 49). When they encounter a new piece of information or a new idea in their field of expertise, they immediately slot it into a fully developed network that enables them to see connections between it and dozens of other things they know. When I encounter a new work in recent British literature, I can immediately see how it connects to other similar works, to major events in British history, to a specific region of Britain, or even to current events there. My students, by contrast, are novice learners in the field; their knowledge of it, to borrow a phrase from *How Learning Works*, is "sparse and superficial" (p. 46). Especially at the beginning of a semester, Ambrose et al. explain, students might "absorb the knowledge from each lecture in a course without connecting the information to other lectures or recognizing themes that cut across the course" (p. 49). They don't know enough about British history to understand that Scotland and England have a complex and fraught history and that therefore we might find connecting threads between Scottish authors in terms of how they write about their neighbors to the south.

In short, they have knowledge, in the sense that they can produce individual pieces of information in specific contexts; what they lack is understanding or comprehension.

And they lack comprehension, even more shortly, because they lack connections.

IN THEORY

James Zull is a biologist whose career took an interesting new turn when he began to reflect on how a better understanding of the biology of the brain could help teachers do their work more effectively. The title of his first book, *The Art of Changing the Brain: Enriching the Practice of Teaching by Exploring the Biology of Learning* (Zull 2002), articulates nicely the major point he wants teachers to understand: when we learn anything new, we are making changes to our brains. When we are helping other people learn new things, like our students, we are making changes to their brains. It would seem only natural, then, that a little bit of understanding of how brains work should accompany our efforts to change them. Since the last science course I took was Concepts in General Science more than 30 years ago, you can imagine how welcome I find books like Zull's, which translate the research of brain researchers into imagery and language accessible to English professors like me.

To understand the link between *making connections* and *building comprehension*, on which this chapter focuses, consider for a moment Zull's depiction of what happens when we learn. Our brains are filled with cells called neurons, which do the work of what we call thinking. A human brain has at least 100 billion neurons, and those neurons contain branching structures called axons that allow them to communicate with other neurons; they do so not by touching the tips of the axons together (as in a handshake) but through the release of chemical neurotransmitters into a tiny space between one neuron and the next called a synaptic gap. As Zull puts it, in his folksy way, neurons "make friends easily" (Zull 2002, p. 96). A single neuron can form literally tens of thousands of connections with other neurons, both near and far away. (The axons can extend as far as six feet.) Neurons form new connections with one another with every new experience we have: new sensations, new thoughts, new actions. As the neurons are connecting to one another in novel ways, growing and strengthening new connections, they are forming networks. The first time neurons link up in a new way, that connection is a temporary or fleeting one; if that connection is used again (because we repeat the thought, or recreate an experience), the link strengthens. The more times the pathway is used, the stronger the connection.

With that brief summary of your brain under our belts, we can now better understand Zull's explanation of how learning constitutes a change in our brain—a change, more particularly, to our neuronal networks: "The knowledge in our minds consists of neuronal networks in our brains, so if that knowledge is to grow, the neuronal networks must physically change. This is the change that a teacher wants to create. It is change in connections. . .unless there is some change in connections, no learning can occur" (Zull 2002, p. 112). According to this definition, we learn when our brains form new neuronal networks or modify existing ones as a result of our experiences; this means that, quite literally, learning requires the continual formation of new connections between our neurons. Think back to the image that Orwell gave us, which now seems quite apt: an individual and isolated piece of knowledge, one that students can't do much with, is exactly like a disconnected islet—just as Dorothy observed in her students. It has few connections to other neuronal networks in our brain. An initial neuronal connection might form when a teacher tells us some piece of information and will fire again in a very small and limited range of circumstances. A piece of knowledge that we understand thoroughly, however, and that we can reflect deeply on and apply to new contexts and more, will have connections to lots of other neuronal networks. It might have come in from the teacher, but then we recognized how it related to something we already knew; we thought about it when we saw something similar in a movie later that day; later still we were able to use it in an essay we were writing. Each of those new uses of that piece of information connected it to another set of networks, until it eventually sits at the heart of a dense weave of connections—what we normally think about as understanding or comprehension. (Readers can find another excellent and more recent presentation of the research on learning-as-neural-connections in the first chapter of Oakley, Rogowsky, and Sejnowski's excellent book *Uncommon Sense Teaching: Practical Insights in Brain Science to Help Students Learn*, which was on press while I was working on the second edition of this book.)

Hence, a simple way of understanding how to build comprehension in our students would be one that consists of helping them forge rich, interconnected networks of knowledge—ones that enable each existing piece of information in our content area to connect with lots of other information, concepts, and ideas. Shifting our language from the biology of the brain to the ways we normally think about student comprehension, we want them to have rich frameworks of knowledge in our content areas, ones that enable them to connect and organize information in meaningful and productive ways. In the past several chapters we have considered how we can help students form and strengthen primary new connections in their brains—creating strong wiring that will allow them to retrieve course content when they need it. In this chapter we consider how we expand those connections into networks that enable students to see the bigger picture, make meaning, apply what they have learned into novel contexts, and more. Our role as teachers now expands as well: we want to facilitate the process of students making connections. As an expert in your discipline, your network is thick with connections. As a teacher in your discipline, your task is to help your students develop a denser, more richly connected network of knowledge and skills in your course content areas.

The more connections student have in a knowledge field, the better they are able to learn and remember new knowledge in that field—which may be the most important reason to emphasize connections in your teaching. This notion is illustrated by a famous little study on memory that was conducted by British psychologists

are making a connection that resonates with you. But your students may have zero interest in the kind of pop culture that fascinates you, and so that connection won't do much for them. When you invite and encourage them to devise their own connections, they will be necessarily more meaningful to them.

MODELS

Strategies to help students modify and enhance their connections can fall at any point during the semester or during any class period. The following five strategies include opportunities for students to activate prior knowledge at the beginning of the semester, to build connected networks throughout the semester with and without technology, and to prepare for final exams and projects as they are finishing the semester. Small teaching here takes the form, not only of brief activities within and outside of the classroom, but also of single-class activities that will help students forge connections within a semester's worth of material.

Connection Notebooks

One of the earliest methods that readers and scholars used to create connections among the things they knew was the commonplace book. A unique combination of diary and scrapbook, commonplace books served as a repository in which people could record passages from their favorite books, treasured quotations and epigrams, inspirational Bible verses, recipes, thoughts, and almost anything else that the person wanted to preserve or remember. They were such a useful and popular item that the English philosopher John Locke authored a guidebook for commonplace-book writers. Commonplace books can serve the same function for students today as they did for people hundreds of years ago—helping them retain and connect what they know and what they are learning. The random juxtapositions that happen when people keep commonplace books not only helps with retention and connection, but it can also spur creative thinking as students see course topics intersecting with other ideas in new and original ways.

I began using a version of the commonplace book, re-christened in my class as *connection notebooks*, while I was completing the first edition of this book. They have since become my favorite small teaching strategy, and they always seem to catch the attention of faculty audiences in the small teaching workshops I give. At the beginning of the semester I hand my students a blue exam book and tell them to bring it to class every day. Once a week, at the end of class, I ask students to take out their connection notebook and write a one-paragraph response to a connection question or prompt I pose to them. Here are some examples of the kinds of questions and prompts I have used:

- How does something you learned in class today connect to something you have learned or discussed in another class, whether it was college or high school or even elementary school?
- Explain one way in which the day's course content manifests itself on campus or in your home lives.
- Can you identify a television show, film, or book that somehow illustrates a course concept from class?
- Describe how today's course material connects to last week's.
- Connect today's course material to a current political or cultural event that's in the news right now.

Sometimes students write their responses to that day's prompt and then class ends, but sometimes we start this activity a few minutes early and I invite a few students to share what they have written before class ends. I collect these notebooks just three times throughout the semester and count them toward a small portion of the course grade. They get full credit for that grade as long as they write me a paragraph. This will be the easiest assignment in this course, I tell them—all you have to do to earn an A on your commonplace book is come to class and write your paragraphs.

The final minutes of class can be a rushed and pointless experience, as we are raising our voices over the clamor of students packing up their things and getting ready to spring for the door. Connection notebooks—which can also be completed online through a discussion board—can slow down those final minutes of class and make them more productive. When you invite your students to make connections in this very deliberate way, you will find yourself surprised at the fascinating connections that students make between your course material and the world around them. But you won't hear those connections—and they might not get made at all—unless you ask for them.

Provide the Framework

As you are introducing new course content to students, especially in the form of course lectures, one way you can help them avoid Orwell's "disconnected islets" is by providing them with the organizing framework of the material and letting them fill in the details. Students are better able to make meaningful connections when they are making them within a visible structure. New learners in a subject tend not to see the structure of a knowledge field—they focus on the details. One way to address this problem in practical terms is to provide students with the outline or framework of your lecture notes and let them fill in the details. This way they can see the larger connections in the field, but they still have to do their own work of making new connections as they listen and observe. Researchers have demonstrated the positive impact of providing such structured (but incomplete) notes in at least two different ways. One experiment compared the exam performance of students who received the full set of lecture notes versus those who received partial notes, and found that the partial-note students performed better on the course final exam (Cornelius and Owen-DeSchryver 2008, p. 8). Another researcher worked with medical students, and again put them into two groups: one group was left to take notes on their own, and the other received guided notes from the instructor, which included "a structured tree map model that identified and summarized the main points of class discussion." Here as well, the researcher found that students who had received the guided notes—with a visual map of the content framework—outperformed the no-notes students on the course exams (Gharravi 2018).

Giving your students guided or structured (but incomplete) notes provides them with the framework of the lecture or reading content, but still forces them to do some of the work of recording ideas and making their own connections. The small teaching strategy here is to help your students make sense of course lectures by providing them with the framework at the outset. You could hand out hard copies of such framework for them to take notes on during class; you could post it to your learning management system so they can take notes on their laptops; or you could simply write the skeletal outline and key terms on the board prior to the start of class. My observations of instructors in multiple disciplines throughout the past 12 years or more has suggested to me that most of us don't think very strategically about the positive role that boards can play in student learning. We tend either to cover them with our notes or to use them to write down ideas or comments that strike us as important in that moment. Setting aside a small section of the board that contains an organizing framework and facilitates students taking meaningful notes and building up rich knowledge networks could help provide some meaning to that kind of impressionistic board use.

Overall, when it comes to providing students with the material from your lecture slides or any other course content, remember that smaller is better; you will help them connect most deeply if you provide only the outline and let them do the rest of the work.

Concept Maps

A rich literature exists on the use of concept maps (also sometimes called mind maps), which present a fast and easy method to help students visualize the organization of key ideas in your course. I like the use of concept maps in particular for group exercises, since group work so often falters when students have not been given a clear task with a concrete outcome, or been given a task that they find too easy or too challenging. The creation of a concept map is a manageable task for a small group of students to undertake at the conclusion of a lesson or a unit of material and offers the additional benefit of being an interesting and (in the best of all possible worlds) even enjoyable activity. The phrase *concept map* essentially describes the activity; Ambrose et al. define a concept map simply as "a visual representation of a knowledge domain" (Ambrose, Bridges, DiPietro, Lovett, and Norman 2010, p. 63). Concept maps can be constructed on sheets of paper, on posters, or on tablets or computers with or without the help of concept-mapping software. One can use concept maps to allow students to construct a visual depiction of everything they know, with key concepts located in boxes or circles in the center of the map and then lines branching off those central concepts or ideas to other subsidiary elements: other concepts, supporting points or details, examples, and so on (think about the image of all those neurons connecting to each other in your brain). The lines between the different elements of a concept map can be labeled in ways that define the relationships between them.

An even better use of concept maps, though, is to provide students with a focus question to which the concept map comes as a response. So a historian might ask students to construct a concept map that demonstrates the positive and negative consequences of violent revolutions; an environmental scientist could assign a concept map that asks students to depict all of the consequences of some major climatological event. I have had my students create concept maps around the major characters in a single novel or around the appearance of a key theme in multiple novels. Even better still, follow the suggestion of *How Learning Works* and have students make multiple maps with different organizing principles. As the authors explain, "Giving students practice organizing their knowledge according to alternative schemata or hierarchies helps them see that different organizations serve different purposes and thus builds more robust and flexible knowledge organizations" (Ambrose, Bridges, DiPietro, Lovett, and Norman 2010, p. 63). If I ask students to create a map of novel characters one day, I might ask them to create one around its themes on a second day and yet another around its images on a third day.

In the early days of my teaching career, I used to have my student groups construct concept maps by giving them blank overheads and asking them to create their maps with dry erase markers; this allowed us to spend the latter part of the class taking a quick look at everyone's maps on the overhead projector. Nowadays, I am more likely to stop at the bookstore before class and pick up some posters and markers and have them create their maps on a larger scale. But you might not prefer these ancient tools of the trade, or you might be teaching in an online environment, or you might have too many students to supervise and display all of the maps produced in your class. Fortunately, a wealth of free concept-mapping programs now exists for your students to create online versions of concept maps. Just search for "free concept mapping," and you will find yourself with more options than you know what to do with. You can find programs to download and save to your device, and you can find websites that allow you to begin creating a new map instantly. Some learning management systems even include concept-mapping options within them, so you might begin by checking there first if you are teaching in a blended or online environment. If your students are accustomed to taking notes on their devices in class, using technological tools for concept mapping will help you keep the activity small without worrying about using things like posters or overheads.

The Minute Thesis

After close to 20 years of teaching, and more than half that time studying and writing about teaching in higher education, I have had exactly one good idea for a teaching strategy that I can't trace back to anywhere else; everything else I have ever recommended, in this book or elsewhere, comes from someone or somewhere else. My single good idea consists of a game called the Minute Thesis, and it represents in some ways the germ of this book, in that it constitutes an ideal small teaching activity: free, easy, and capable of use in any size class, for any length of time you wish, from 10 minutes to the full class period. I began using it about 12 years ago as an attempt to help students at the end of the semester see connections across the various works we had read in an effort to develop ideas for their final papers—which mostly, in my classes, require them to do comparative analyses of several works from the course reading list. I wrote the name of the seven novels we had read on the board in a single column; in a second column, I wrote a list of themes that we had seen in various novels throughout the semester. I handed a marker to a student in the front row, asked her to walk up to the board and circle a single theme, and then asked her to draw lines connecting that theme to two different novels. Then I invited all students to spend 1 minute thinking about a thesis for an argument that would explain how those two novels connected to that theme. Some of them stared off into space, thinking; some of them actually wrote a phrase or sentence in their notebooks. After a minute (maybe two), I asked them to tell me what they had come up with. A brief silence ensued (this always happens); then a tentative hand arose, and a tentative student made a tentative statement. I praised the student's idea and asked for another. More hands arose, more confidently, and more ideas emerged. After 5–10 minutes listening to the fascinating new set of connections that were emerging, I stopped the discussion and handed the marker to another student, asking him to circle a new theme and connect it to two different novels; the process then began anew. Over the course of a class period, the students created dozens of brief thesis statements that connected the novels and themes of the course in new and interesting ways, and many of the students took an idea they expressed in that class period and developed it into their final paper.

This brief little activity occurs in the final week of every class I teach now, as a way to help students solidify existing connections they have developed or envision new ones as they are preparing for their final papers or projects or the final exam. The potential variations in how you might conduct it are endless, as are the ways technology could modify or enhance it. You could, for example, use your course learning management system to start a handful of discussion threads that pair various course elements in different ways and ask each student to contribute a one-sentence thesis to that discussion thread over the course of a 24-hour period; to push their thinking even further, you might then assign students to articulate what the supporting evidence would look like under someone else's thesis. In the classroom you could likewise play out each iteration of the Minute Thesis further by selecting one thesis from those initially proffered and spending 10 minutes spelling out what the argument might look like. Or you could use three columns instead of two, requiring the students to think even more creatively about how to see the course material in newly connected ways. All that's really required is that you or the students set up columns or categories of essential course concepts or texts, connect them in new and creative ways, and then ask the students to describe how or why those connections make sense (or even don't make sense). In this way, just as in the practice of giving students an outline and key terms and letting them fill in their notes, you are offering the scaffolding through the columns or categories but then requiring students to make the connections themselves.

One final benefit of the Minute Thesis is that it can help students gain some practice in what might seem to them the mysterious process of coming up with new or original ideas—something we frequently ask of them when we assign papers or presentations or research projects. What we typically think about as "original" thinking usually means forging new connections between things that have not been connected before (Lang 2013, pp. 192–205). Ideas almost always have lineages, and those lineages can help us see the key role that creative connections play in the process of generating new thinking. Playing the Minute Thesis demystifies the process of coming up with new connections, and gives the students a tool they can use in all of their classes when they are trying to brainstorm ideas for their assignments.

Examples, Analogies, Reasons

I'll wrap up the models of this chapter with a more general recommendation for how to keep connections at the forefront of your thinking about teaching. You will help your students expand and grow their knowledge if you give them prompts and structured opportunities to make connections. No matter what your class looks like, seek regularly to prompt students to respond in some way—through writing, class discussion, paired conversation, polling, and more—with the following three questions:

- Can you give me an example?
- What's it similar to? Or different from?
- Why should we care about it?

These questions will encourage students to make connections through examples, analogies, and reasons—all of which should contribute to deepening their learning. Build these questions into your practice and use them to keep students engaged and thinking throughout your course.

PRINCIPLES

Connection exercises provide a bridge between your expert comprehension of your subject matter and the novice understanding of your students. As you consider how to help your students create their own connections, keep that primary focus in mind. You are helping your students obtain the big-picture view that informs and animates your own grasp of the material.

Provide the Framework. Remember that one of the most important ways your knowledge of the course content differs from your students lies in your ability to organize and connect concepts and information in meaningful ways. As you encounter new knowledge in your field, you can remember and work with it because of that organization. New learners in a field initially need lots of help in seeing the framework or organization of the material to be learned. You can help them by making the framework as visible as possible, pointing them back to it frequently, and helping them recognize where new material fits into the frame. The more familiar the students become with your course content, the less of this you will have to do.

Facilitate Connections. The network of connections in your head doesn't transfer wholly into the heads of your students. Providing the frame to your students not only will help them better understand the organization of knowledge in your field but will also leave open the space for them to create the connections in their brains that will fuel deep learning. Be creative in developing techniques that allow students to see unexpected juxtapositions, chart new pathways through the material, or invent their own new knowledge networks. Be present as the guide and expert who can provide feedback on their discoveries, and help nudge them in productive new directions when they get stuck or stray too far from what you know works for experts in the field.

Leverage Peer Learning Power. Of all the small teaching techniques considered in this book, this one lends itself most easily to the use of groups or peer learning activities. Your students all share the position of being novice learners in your field and can help each other understand how to build bridges between those disconnected islets. When you are providing opportunities for students to create connections, allow and encourage them to help each other. The process of creating connections lends itself to collaborative exercises that can revitalize the classroom and inject some fun into learning. The days on which we play the Minute Thesis game are always the most enjoyable ones of the semester; the room fills with energy and curiosity as the students make their own connections and consider the connections made by their peers.

SMALL TEACHING QUICK TIPS: CONNECTING

Making new connections is more complex than retrieving a remembered piece of information, so you may need to set aside more space and time in your course plans for connection exercises. Rather than trying to squeeze them into five- or ten-minute sessions in class, see if you can allot them more time in single-class sessions at the opening, midway point, or closing of the semester.

- Use connection notebooks to help your students connect that day's course content to some aspect of their lives or experiences outside of the classroom. Make the notebooks a very low-stakes assessment activity—and enjoy seeing all of the fascinating connections your students make.
- Consider providing students only with the scaffolding or framework of lecture material in advance of class; let them fill in the framework with their own connections.
- Ask students to create concept maps that answer questions or solve problems. Use concept maps multiple times throughout the semester with different organizational principles.
- Consider using the Minute Thesis or other in-class activities that help students see or create new connections prior to major assignments or exams.
- Build into your teaching approach frequent opportunities for students to come up with their own examples, analogies, and reasons.

CONCLUSION

In *A Clergyman's Daughter*, protagonist Dorothy Hare discovers an ingenious method for connecting the disconnected islets of her students' minds in their history lessons:

She bought a roll of cheap plain wallpaper at an uphol-sterer's shop, and set the children to making an historical chart. They marked the roll of paper into centuries and years, and struck scraps that they cut out of illustrated papers—pictures of knights in armour and Spanish galle-ons and printing presses and railway trains—at the appro-priate places. Pinned around the walls of the room, the chart presented, as the scraps grew in number, a sort of panorama of English history. (p. 222)

This active learning strategy of Dorothy's incorporates just about everything we have considered in this chapter: providing a structure that helps students see the big picture (the chart), hav-ing them fill in the connections across and between the elements of that big picture (the historical dates), and inviting them to bring in new connections from outside of the class (the illustrated papers). With the help of this simple framework provided by the teacher, Dorothy's students begin truly learning.

Chapter 5

Practicing

INTRODUCTION

In spring 2007, I taught a course on contemporary British literature to a class of mostly junior and senior students. To supplement the novels and plays and poems we were reading with some broader cultural context, I asked each student to give a 10–15-minute presentation to the class on a British work of art in a popular genre. They could offer presentations on films, television shows, or even their favorite music. I thought the assignment would elicit some strong work since it gave students the opportunity to present on topics in which they were interested—one student selected Pink Floyd's *The Wall*, another did the BBC television series *The Office*, and so on. Leading up to the days on which the presentations occurred, I gave the students a few tips on effective presentation techniques, enjoined them to practice at least two or three times before the final classes, and worked with some of them individually on the structure and organization of their material. I had high hopes, which were painfully dashed on presentation day. The students had clearly not practiced or timed their presentations out. The slides were poorly designed and crammed with text—which the students often read out word for word. The students were either nervous and stilted or overly casual and unpracticed. The presentations were supposed to last 10–12 minutes;

one student spoke for more than 30, despite frequent injunctions to wrap things up. In fact, their work was so poor that I decided afterward I would never ask my students to give presentations again. I just couldn't stand the thought of sitting through another set of them.

However, in fall 2008, I agreed to teach a course in our honors program in which juniors produce a proposal for a thesis they will write during their senior year. The program requires that these juniors finish the course with an oral defense of their proposal—which meant that, just a semester after taking my no-presentation vow, I was stuck once again with observing and evaluating end-of-semester presentations. The stakes were now raised: each student in the class worked with a faculty mentor, who was asked to attend the defenses. These presentations would thus take place in front of an audience of my peers. In part because of these raised stakes, and in part because of my previous experiences with presentations, I decided that I simply could not bear to sit through another set of unpracticed, ill-prepared, poorly timed rambles. I had to do something to better prepare the students to succeed at these presentations. Unfortunately, I have no degree in public speaking and have never taught speech, so I didn't feel qualified to give detailed instructions on the finer points of designing presentations or public speaking. At the same time, I speak a lot in public. I do this not only as a professor speaking to students, but also as a frequent guest speaker at faculty development workshops, or lectures on other campuses. The one thing I have learned from that experience has been the value of repeated practice. The more times I give a specific lecture, or even mini lecture, the better it gets. Before I unveil any new material at a workshop, I have usually delivered it to my cat or to an empty classroom at least once or twice. As I have gained more experience as a speaker, I rely less on these practice sessions, but even now I still will usually run through the opening five minutes of a presentation at least two or three times.

This seemed to me like a gift I could give to my students as they prepared for their presentations. So as the final weeks of the semester in this honors class approached, I made an announcement to the students: "On the class before the presentations begin, you must be prepared to give the first two minutes of your presentation to the class. That's it—just the first two minutes. Rehearse it and be ready." With 15 students in a 75-minute class, and figuring time for transition and critique, that meant I had to give up one whole class period to this practice session—no content that day at all, just helping them improve their presentations. Given my previous experiences with the poor quality of student presentations, I was not at all sure that the effort would be worth the lost time. I still had no particular advice in mind to offer; my only real goal was to force the students to rehearse a few times, after which I hoped they would recognize the value of their rehearsals and do some additional practicing on their own.

Rehearsal day arrived. I selected a volunteer and asked the first student to begin. I let her speak for about three sentences, which were stiff and clearly memorized, before I stopped her.

"Hang on a second," I said. "Start over."

"Did I do something wrong?"

"Nope. I just want you to start over."

She began again, speaking a little more confidently. I let her go another few sentences.

"Wait," I said, interrupting again. She wore a pained expression. Students were looking at me, and at one another, with bewilderment.

"You're not doing anything wrong," I said. "But just start over again for me."

A chill descended on the room at that moment, as students began to wonder why I was torturing this poor woman. Her third time around was much better, as she found her way into her own words, so I let her continue for a while. At the end of some technical explanation she gave about her material, I asked her to stop and describe it for me in her own words without looking at her notes. She put down her notes and broke out of the rigid posture in which she had been standing to explain what she meant. It came out a hundred times more clearly.

"That's better," I said. "Say it like that in the presentation."

"OK," she said, and then resumed her presentation where she had left off.

"No, no," I interrupted. "Say it like that *right now* in the presentation."

"Go back and do it again?" she said.

"Yes, go back and do it again. And don't look at your notes."

And so it went for the next 70 minutes, as I asked student after student to repeat false starts, clear up technical material or jargon, and put away written notes. The room went from a climate of fear and anxiety to one of laughter and relaxation as the students picked up on what was happening and saw that all I was trying to teach them were the virtues of practice and rehearsal. I can't say there were not a few bad moments. One student was so nervous and stammering it was painful to watch, and I thought interrupting her would do more harm than good. So I just let her talk. Eventually she realized that nobody was going to rescue her, and she locked in and worked her way through her nerves. The following week the students gave their presentations, and they were, by far, the best student talks I have ever seen. It could not have been clearer that every one of them had gone back to their rooms and rehearsed and timed themselves until they had it right. Some were better than others, but even the worst would have beaten out almost any presentation I had seen before.

IN THEORY

College classes frequently operate in a strange fashion if we think of them in contrast to other pursuits that human beings attempt to master. A professor spends a semester lecturing to her students about some complex subject matter. A good professor mixes those lectures with some active-learning strategies such as discussions and group exercises. But mostly in class the students are listening or talking. Then the first midterm period rolls around, and now the students are doing something quite different from listening or talking: they are writing essays, or answering multiple-choice questions, or designing presentations, or doing a variety of other complex cognitive activities that are distinct from the simple acts of talking or listening. If we taught students to play soccer in this way, it would entail putting them into the stands at a soccer game, lecturing to them about soccer, and encouraging them to have discussions about it. Then we might have them do a bunch of calisthenics. Then we would stick them in a stadium full of fans and tell them to play soccer. I suspect you would enjoy watching that soccer game about as much as I enjoyed watching my student presentations before I taught that honors class.

The small teaching strategy to be recommended in this chapter lies at the heart of this section and the heart of the book as a whole:

> Students should have frequent opportunities to practice *in class* whatever cognitive skills that you want them to master, and that you will be assessing for a grade.

The trick in this recommendation lies in how specifically you identify the intellectual skills of that *whatever*. It may seem to you that holding an in-class discussion about a text serves as good preparation for writing an essay about that text. Those are two different things, though. To sit and listen to a discussion, contemplate ideas, and occasionally lob out one of your own constitutes something radically distinct from sitting down with an idea, parsing it out into pieces that can be separated into paragraphs, marshalling evidence for each paragraph, and so on. "It is virtually impossible to become proficient at a mental task," writes cognitive psychologist Daniel Willingham, "without extended practice" (Willingham 2014, p. 107). If we want students to become proficient at the specific mental tasks that we are planning to assess—such as writing formal essays or responding to essay exam questions, writing lab reports, taking multiple-choice or true–false or short-answer exams—we have to give them extended practice at those tasks. Each of these types of assessments, and any other type of assessment you can dream up, requires students mastering a specific set of cognitive processes—none of them are exactly like any other. Students, like the rest of us, can demonstrate real mastery of one type of cognitive process while having little skill with a related one. You will perhaps know this from your experience meeting and working with students who can think very quickly on their feet in class discussions but can't write very well, or those who can write brilliant essays but rarely make substantive contributions to class discussions. This point was driven home to me firmly the year after I taught the honors class, and became the director of the honors program, where I began teaching the writing-intensive introductory course for the program's first-year students. Sometimes I would read the poorly-written essays of a particular student and wonder how on earth she had been admitted to the program with such poor writing skills; then later on I would learn from one of my colleagues that she was brilliant at mathematics or science. My unspoken assumption had been that the really smart and talented students would be able to quickly master any cognitive challenge we threw at them; my experience did not bear out this assumption.

Neither does the research of cognitive psychologists or learning theorists. "As far as anyone knows," writes Willingham in *Why Don't Students Like School?*, "the only way to develop mental facility [at a cognitive task] is to repeat the target process again and again" (Willingham 2014, p. 115). The first edition of *Small Teaching* contained several pages of theoretical support for this claim, but in this second edition I have trimmed that material significantly. In the talks and workshops I have given for faculty over the past five years I have discovered that most people grasp this point readily, especially when they reflect upon their own experiences both as learners and teachers. Most of us have had the experience of having to practice something again and again in order to get it right, whether that is swinging a tennis racket or learning to cook or even making use of a particular teaching strategy. To get it right, we have to do it many times: trying, making mistakes, correcting them, and trying again. Most of us have also had experiences similar to the one I describe in the introduction to this chapter: witnessing smart and capable students failing miserably at some novel task that we assumed they should be able to master just because they had been able to complete some related but different kind of task. Many readers have actually reported to me that they have had similar experiences with student presentations in particular.

But I still want to address a common response that is given by faculty who accept the idea that students should have multiple opportunities to practice whatever cognitive skills we expect them to demonstrate on our assessments, but who are still reluctant to dedicate class time to such activities. According to these faculty, that's what homework is for. Why should I devote my valuable class time, they wonder, to allowing students to work on writing grammatically correct sentences or developing core math skills or answering multiple-choice questions or giving pieces of their presentations? Why can't I give them the instruction they need to practice those tasks and then send them off to complete that practice on their own? Aren't we just coddling students and wasting class time if we draw such practice activities into the classroom, even if we are doing so—as I will recommend—in the 10–15-minute periods that are the hallmark of small teaching?

To answer these questions, we have to dig a little more deeply into the idea of practice and consider the work of Harvard psychologist Ellen Langer. Decades of Langer's research on cognition and learning are distilled in a brief but wonderful book called *The Power of Mindful Learning*. Langer's concept of *mindful learning* can help those of us who teach understand that there are really two challenges when it comes to practice in the classroom: ensuring that students do it, and ensuring that students do it *well*. Orchestrating opportunities for students to practice a skill is essential, but of course we want to make sure that their practice is effective: that it locks in the essential skills, helps them apply those skills in different contexts, and provides a foundation for future skill development. Not all practice will do that. Mindless repetition of an activity, which might look like practice, can actually lead to what Langer calls *overlearning*, in which we engage in some activity so frequently that we continue to practice it in the same way over and over again, even when circumstances change and call for adjustments. Many years ago, when I first learned to ski and did so frequently, skis had the same width at the back end and the middle as they did at the front end. Fifteen years later, when I began skiing again after a long hiatus, skis had changed: now they are shaped, which means that they widen at the front and back—and that executing turns as you ski down the mountain requires a different set of bodily movements. I knew this because someone had told it to me, but I still couldn't figure out how to do it. I just kept doing what I had always done, fighting against the shape of my skis—not because I wasn't trying but because I couldn't understand how to move my body differently. I had overlearned my ski habits and could not adjust them to the new circumstances of my shaped skis. Langer's research suggests that the same thing can happen with the cognitive tasks we give to our students. Asking them to drill the same tasks over and over again on their homework puts them on autopilot and prevents them from refining and further developing their skills in the way that experts continually do.

Langer's theory of mindful learning provides a pathway to practice that enhances learning but doesn't lead to such over-learning. She defines a mindful approach to learning as having three characteristics: "the continuous creation of new categories; openness to new information; and an implicit awareness of more than one perspective" (Langer 2007, p. 4). First, the learner must be willing to shift and develop the categories that will guide her through a cognitive task. If the learner is using Theory A to guide her through a problem-solving session and finds herself stuck in a dead end, she should have the ability to recognize that Theory A might need modification or even need chucking out and replacing with Theory B. A mindful learner cannot simply plug and chug formulae, in other words. Second, the learner must be attentive to new information that might be blocked from view by her usual approach. A rote learner will complete a task the same way every time, not noticing variations in the landscape or challenges within the problem that might help her further develop her skill levels. Mindful learners get in the habit of pulling their heads up and looking around to see what they might be missing. Finally, the mindful learner recognizes that perspectives are always limited and that final conclusions are always provisional. She accepts the possibility that new and better approaches to a problem might yet arise, and she remains open to the potential value of perspectives she doesn't inhabit. The three components of mindful learning, taken together, represent both activity and attitude: the activity involves monitoring and questioning one's approach to a routine problem or challenge; the attitude involves openness to the possibility of change.

I was nudged into mindful learning on the slopes by a friend of mine who had undergone the same shift I had from straight to shaped skis. He pointed out several small body movements that I was doing incorrectly, so with his advice in mind I became a much more deliberate skier. I had to think more carefully about what I was doing as I carved my turns down the mountain, and I learned to pay much closer attention to what my hips were doing, accept feedback from my body and the terrain, and make continual adjustments. Over time, I had to do less and less of that, as the new habits became more automatic to me. There are two essential points here. First, I am now a much more thoughtful skier than I ever was and enjoy the challenges of approaching and navigating different terrains in ways that I had lost when I was just thoughtlessly whizzing down the mountain. Second, even though I learned to ski more mindfully, I still had to engage in constant practice in order to master this new skill. If anything, the need for me to engage in more mindful skiing inspired me to practice even more than I otherwise would have, when I was locked into unproductive patterns. Becoming a mindful practitioner made my practice more interesting, and paved the way for it to work.

The theory of mindful learning might help you in your work and leisure habits as it helped me with my skiing. But our real challenge is to put this theory into practice in the classroom: How do you help students mindfully practice the skills you want them to obtain? Consider, for the last time, my skiing example. In that case a more experienced skier pointed out what I was doing wrong and still will occasionally ski behind me and give me a pointer here and there if I ask him to. He observed my practice, gave me feedback on what I was doing, and then continued to monitor my progress and be available when I got stuck or had questions. The importance of his presence during my practice finally leads us back to the question I posed previously: why can't we just provide students with instruction and then send them off to practice on their own? Because doing so will leave them open to the possibility that they practice mindlessly, overlearning skills or developing poor habits instead of engaging with the task in the kind of mindful ways promoted by Langer. If you are present when they are engaged in their practice, however, you can play the role of my skiing friend: you can provide feedback while they are working, you can occasionally ask them to pause and reflect upon what they are doing, and you can offer suggestions for creative new pathways that they might try when they get stuck on a problem. You, in other words, are the best guide that students have toward mindful learning and toward practicing in ways that promote mindful learning—but you will best serve as that guide when you are present to them during their practice, whether that means standing in the room with them or interacting with them online.

Even though this still might sound like a complex task, don't overthink it (bad advice to give academics, I know). The models of this chapter will walk you through the core steps. Just to demonstrate how simple it can be to help learners engage in more mindful practice, though, consider an experiment conducted by Langer and two colleagues designed to test whether they could help students learn to practice the piano mindfully. Two groups of musical novices were given some simple exercises to practice on the piano and then a 20-minute lesson on a specific piece; afterward, their playing was taped and evaluated by experts. The first group was simply instructed to do the exercises and enjoined to practice them in the traditional way: through repetition and rote learning. The second group was given this instruction:

We would like you to try to learn these fingering exercises without relying on rote memorization. Try to keep learning new things about your piano playing. Try to change your style every few minutes, and not lock into one particular pattern. While you practice, attend to the context, which may include very subtle variations or any feelings, sensations, or thoughts you are having. (Langer 2007, p. 27)

The students in the second group were given one additional reminder about these instructions at the midway point of their practice sessions. When the two groups' playing was evaluated afterward by experts, the results confirmed the power of mindful practice: "The subjects given mindful instruction in the early steps of piano playing were rated as more competent and more creative and also expressed more enjoyment of the activity" (p. 27). If you are capable of opening your student practice sessions with instructions like the ones provided by Langer and her colleagues and of pausing students occasionally throughout the process—whether you do so individually or to the group as a whole—you are capable of helping students learn through mindful practice in your classroom.

MODELS

The models presented here will deviate slightly from the form established in the other chapters because the strategy is such a straightforward and obvious one and has been stated already: you should give students small and regular opportunities in class (or synchronously online) to practice whatever cognitive skills you would like them to develop and that they will need to succeed on your assessments. They should be able to practice these tasks in advance of and separate from formal grading, and they should receive some feedback on their practice, from you or from peers. Instead of repeating this advice in different forms, I instead outline the three steps that are essential to creating this type of practice session.

Unpack Your Assessments

Your first task is to analyze your assessments and to break them down into the various cognitive tasks that they will require of your students and to understand for yourself the priorities that you assign to those tasks when you grade the assessments. Only after you have unpacked the assessments in this way can you determine what will be most beneficial for your students to practice in class. Once you have done this, you might find it surprising to note—as I once did—how many of the skills that you require of students on your assessments are ones you don't normally allow them to practice in your course.

For example, writing a paper of literary analysis, which most of us who teach literature ask of our students, obviously requires students to analyze and make an argument about a work of literature. That's the skill that we typically focus on in class: we model the process of analyzing literature for them, and we ask them to venture their own analyses in our class discussions or group exercises. But consider just a small number of some of the *other* cognitive skills that are necessary to write an effective paper of literary analysis and that would come into play in my evaluation of such a paper:

- Writing an introductory paragraph
- Crafting a one- or two-sentence argumentative thesis
- Incorporating quotations into an essay
- Building body paragraphs around evidence
- Writing according to correct grammatical conventions
- Writing a concluding paragraph

Looking over this (partial) list of skills my students would need to complete this complex assignment, I would probably pinpoint the second, third, and fourth ones as accounting for the highest proportion of the grade I will assign to their essays. In a typical class session in a literature course, I might give them some form of practice for the second skill by asking them to argue or state their positions about the work we are discussing—although even this I would typically do orally instead of in writing. However, until I encountered Langer's work and thought about the importance of mindful practice in the classroom, I almost never gave my students time in class to develop the skill of building a paragraph around a piece of evidence or of incorporating a quotation effectively into a piece of writing. Post-Langer, I now have students complete writing exercises in which they practice these skills several times in a semester.

Consider the more generic example of asking students to give a slide-based presentation: putting aside whatever cognitive tasks might be required by the specific dictates of your presentation assignment or the work of your discipline, such an assignment entails the following cognitive activities:

- Organizing material into slide-sized chunks
- Creating slides with an appropriate amount of text
- Finding, selecting, and incorporating images, video, or audio onto slides
- Balancing their spoken words with the text on the slides
- Allowing enough time for audience members to absorb the material on each slide

If you have sat through presentations at your disciplinary conferences, as I am sure most of us have, you will no doubt recognize that these are complex skills that many teachers have not yet mastered, much less students. How many times have you seen, for example, slides that are totally jam-packed with text that is then read out verbatim by the presenter? Or how many times have you seen slides that are totally jam-packed with text that are projected for less time than it would take for the audience member to read them? Did you know that research has been conducted on this very issue of whether or not we should read the text on our slides (Miller 2014, p. 154)? And if you don't specifically give students practice at creating and speaking from slides—based either on that research or on your own experience as a deliverer of presentations or as someone who has witnessed many of them—how are you expecting your students to do it effectively? And how fair is it to grade them on it?

I know that a common (if unspoken) objection to this line of thinking might be that the students should have learned and have practiced these skills somewhere else: in their composition courses, or in a speech class, or in high school, or in someone else's class. Maybe. But unless your students are walking into your class and nailing their presentations from day one, they obviously still need practice at it. If you are not going to give them that practice, whom do you expect to do it?

> First step: break down your major assessments as finely as you can, and identify the cognitive skills that students would need to succeed on that assessment.

Parcel Them Out and Practice Them

> Second step: create small teaching opportunities for your students to practice those cognitive skills in class or online.

Practice strikes me as an especially appropriate activity to assign to the closing 10–15 minutes of class, as your practice session can help the students work on skills that stem from that day's class material. If we are having an open-ended discussion about a poem in my literature course, in which both I and the students have articulated various thesis-type ideas about what we think the poem means, I could close that discussion 10 minutes before the end of class and ask students to write two sample thesis statements in their notebooks about the poem based on the arguments they heard that day. Even better, I could close the class 15 minutes early, spend 5 minutes reviewing with them the components that make for an effective argumentative thesis, and *then* ask them to take 10 minutes and write two sample thesis statements. At the beginning of the next class session, before we moved onto new material, I might ask them to select one of the two thesis statements they crafted, find a quote from the poem that would support it, and then write a single body paragraph centered on that quote. (Again, ideally, I would perhaps spend just a couple of minutes beforehand reminding them about the essential components of a good body paragraph.) Giving students a dozen such in-class tasks over the course of the semester would provide them with substantial practice at skills they need for many types of college essay assignments.

For a presentation assignment, you might pick a day two weeks in advance of the actual presentations and ask students to bring their laptops to class. In the final 10 minutes of a class in which you present some new material to them, ask them to pair up and work together on the creation of a single slide designed to teach an audience about Concept A. In the following class sessions, allot the final 10 minutes of each class to asking a handful of students to stand up and give a 2-minute presentation of the slide they created. Better yet, as in the writing example, make it the final 15 minutes and spend the first 5 minutes reminding them that reading text directly from slides can produce something called the *redundancy effect*, which can reduce learning, but that too much difference between what's on the slide and what they say also has been shown to reduce learning. So they should be searching for what Michelle Miller describes as the "'Goldilocks' principle with respect to the discrepancy between the narration and the visually presented slide"—they should clearly reference and highlight the key components of what they have put on the slide, but not simply read it out directly (Miller 2014, p. 154). Giving students the opportunity to create several practice slides, and then to work on speaking those slides to an audience, would go a long way toward improving the majority of student presentations I have seen.

Provide Feedback

Third step: provide feedback on their practice efforts.

The ideal practice–feedback situation is something like what I encountered with my more experienced skiing friend—while I practiced, he observed and offered timely suggestions on how to improve. This kind of feedback can occur in individual tutoring sessions, in coaching many kinds of sports, and in arts instruction—think of a student practicing the piano under the watchful eye of her instructor. Although we obviously can't create this kind of one-on-one feedback loop in our typical college courses, we still should search for ways to provide students with feedback on their practice. The simplest means of doing so, in a face-to-face classroom, is to combine individual and group feedback during and after the practice session. While students are engaged in their practice work, circulate among them and offer individual feedback on the work of as many students as you can.

You will probably find that patterns of problems begin to emerge as you observe the work of more and more students. After you have offered some individual feedback, then, you can pause the session and offer feedback on those common issues to the entire group. This process can be repeated as often as necessary. At the start of such a practice session, you will have to make clear that you intend to provide feedback in this manner. If you don't, you might find that some students feel uncomfortable at receiving feedback in this way, thinking that you are singling them out for some reason. Just announce at the start of your first session that you will be circulating and offering feedback to as many students as you can and using what you observe to help the entire group.

Obviously, you can do the same thing in online environments, offering individualized or spot feedback on practice work and then using what you observed to offer more general remarks to the whole class. If you do use this method to offer feedback, either face-to-face or online, it's worth a few minutes of reflection on how you can spread the individualized feedback around the entire room so that as many people as possible receive individualized attention over the course of the whole semester. You can use the shape of the room, the rows or columns of desks, or even the course roster to help ensure you are circulating among the students in an equitable way.

Finally, although much of the feedback you give to students might offer simple tweaks or tips on how to accomplish a particular task more effectively, you can certainly shape that feedback so that it pushes students toward the kind of mindful learning Langer advocates. In the provocative closing chapters of *The Power of Mindful Learning*, she makes the case that the kind of open-ended, flexible thinking fostered by mindful learning constitutes the very heart of what we think about as intelligence:

Although flexible thinking is the essence of mindfulness, flexibility can also be considered a quality of intelligent thinking. We all have a repertoire of lower-level procedures and higher-level strategies that may be tried in novel settings. The larger our repertoire and the less we are attached to any specific procedure or strategy, the more flexible our thinking is likely to be...Our general capacity to sort through these various strategies and procedures and assess which can be applied most appropriately to a novel task is the process usually called intelligent thinking. (p. 113)

In other words, intelligence in the completion of cognitive tasks consists of the ability to step back from our familiar patterns, consider whether alternatives exist, and then recognize whether any of those alternatives might work more effectively. So if we want students to think in these intelligent and creative ways about the cognitive tasks required by our assessments, we should encourage them to do so in our practice sessions. Feedback might occasionally nudge them to step back from the specific task and consider alternatives. Why have you chosen to use that strategy for your introduction? What alternatives might you have chosen? Is that the only formula that you could have used to solve this problem? Have you ever encountered a question like this outside of this course? How did you answer it then? If I posed this question to someone who had not taken this course, how do you think they would go about trying to answer it? Questions like these, designed to push thinkers up to a more aerial view of their practice, may help create the kind of mindful learners that don't lock into familiar patterns and rely on rote repetition to complete their cognitive tasks.

PRINCIPLES

As Ellen Langer's theory of mindful learning reminds us, not all practice is alike. But any opportunity you give your students to practice cognitive activities in your classroom will likely yield them benefits when they are faced with completing your assessments. Keep in mind the following principles as you reflect on how to incorporate effective practice sessions into your course.

Make Time for In-Class Practice. While you certainly can and should give students practice opportunities through homework, make time for it in your classroom or (for online courses) synchronous sessions. Practice that takes place away from the presence of an instructor can become a breeding ground for overlearning, mindless repetition, and the development of wrong or poor habits. Practice that takes place with the benefit of your presence and feedback has potential to create more powerful learning. Keeping the sessions small will help you find space for them in your valuable classroom time.

Space It Out. According to the research we reviewed on spacing and interleaving, five 10-minute practice sessions spaced out throughout a course will work more effectively than a single 50-minute practice session. This makes practicing according to the small teaching paradigm ideal for learning: the multiple, brief sessions a small teaching approach would recommend are exactly what should benefit your students most fully.

Practice Mindfully. Repetition helps us master cognitive tasks in the same way that it helps us master learning to cook a favorite dish, skiing on shaped skis, or speaking confidently in front of an audience. Although repetition on its own will produce a certain base level of competency, it won't help us grow and improve unless we pause at least occasionally to reflect on what we are doing, why we are doing it, and whether alternative pathways might exist. Use practice sessions to nudge students toward mindful learning.

SMALL TEACHING QUICK TIPS: PRACTICE

Much of the work of this small teaching technique happens outside of the classroom, as you analyze the assessments you give and break them down into their component skill parts. Once you have done that, make a little space in class for each of them and guide your students toward mindful learning.

- Before the semester begins, brainstorm a comprehensive list of cognitive skills your students will need to develop to succeed in your course.
- Prioritize them; decide which ones students will need to develop most immediately and which ones can emerge only after they have mastered some basic skills.
- Review your course schedule and decide where you can make space for small practice sessions in key skills prior to your major assessments; mark those sessions on the syllabus schedule.
- Stick to your plan. Prior to any major assessment, ensure that students have had multiple opportunities to practice the skills they will need to do well, from creating slides or writing paragraphs to answering multiple-choice questions.

CONCLUSION

As you can probably tell from the examples I gave throughout this chapter, incorporating brief practice sessions into the classroom has been one of the most important changes I have made to my teaching in recent years. After the success I had in helping students give more effective presentations, I began moving more and more skill-based activities into the classroom, including everything from writing introductory paragraphs to writing sample essay exam questions. All of that practice, along with the positive effects that appeared in the work of my students, convinced me completely of its potential to improve student learning and performance.

I can't close this chapter without noting one hurdle that I had to overcome as I gradually shifted more and more practice sessions into my classroom: the uneasy feeling I would get when students were working away at some task and I wasn't actively engaged in what I had always thought about as teaching. I wasn't lecturing them, leading a discussion, trying to keep a handle on a group project, or supervising an assessment. These are comfortable and familiar activities for teachers; observing, listening, and reflecting seem less familiar to us in the classroom. However, if you can learn to use the time in which they are practicing as an opportunity for you to gain a better understanding of their current skill levels and can offer them both individualized and group feedback, you will grow more accustomed to those moments in which you are not teaching in more familiar ways, just as your students will grow more accustomed to thinking about the classroom space not as a place to sit passively and absorb material, but as a site in which to engage in active, mindful practice of important intellectual skills.

Chapter 6

Explaining

INTRODUCTION

I suspect you could theoretically survive parenting a child without ever raising your voice in anger—an achievement I certainly can't claim to have made. All the restraint you may have demonstrated in the early years of parenting, however, will melt when your child begins learning to drive, and you find yourself in the passenger seat of a terrifying death machine with a 16-year-old at the helm. No matter how carefully they have studied the rules of the road and practiced in parking lots, 16-year-olds who are learning to drive do things like ignore yield signs or forget to look in both directions before pulling out into traffic. At those moments you can choose either to raise your voice or to crash.

I have chosen to raise my voice.

However justified I may have felt in barking an emergency instruction in potentially hazardous driving situations, my children never seemed to appreciate the value of what I was doing for us both (i.e., saving our lives). This meant that driving lessons in the Lang household, which were happily coming to a close while I was finishing this second edition, typically consisted of tension-filled rides around the neighborhood in which I was continually on the verge of boiling over and my children were continually on the verge of tears. During the time when I was supervising these white-knuckled drives with my second-oldest daughter, I also happened to be doing some reading about self-explanation and learning, the basic premise of which is that *learners benefit from explaining out loud (to themselves or a teacher) what they are doing during the completion of a learning task.* Less to improve her learning than to diffuse the tension in the car, I began asking my daughter to tell me about what she was doing as she drove. One of her problems had been that she tended to drive too close to the right side of the road, perhaps out of an exaggerated (and understandable) concern for not drifting into oncoming traffic. When I asked her to talk about what she was doing as she drove, she noticed this issue herself, about which I had reminded her earlier (like a thousand times), and she made a self-correction. She navigated more to the center of the road. This happened several other times with other driving tasks. Whenever I asked her to explain what she was doing, she would analyze her own driving in ways that didn't seem to happen when she was just sitting there attempting to navigate the road and waiting for me to shout at her.

This helpful incident was my first real observation of the power of explaining, a learning strategy that can assist students in a variety of different ways. In the first edition of *Small Teaching,* I focused this chapter on the idea of *self-explaining*: speaking or writing to yourself (or to an instructor) about your learning as it happens. Prompting my daughter to explain what she was doing as she learned to drive (and why she was doing it) would fall into this category. As we shall see below, some excellent research suggests that self-explaining can help learners master skills they are trying to develop. But in this second edition I have broadened the scope of this learning activity to include the idea of *explaining* more generally. The research base on the power of explaining to promote learning takes the form of studies which demonstrate that when students are asked to teach something to other students, or even just asked to prepare to teach something to other people, they learn it more deeply than if they were asked to study the material for an exam or other assessment. Explaining your newly learned skills or content aloud, to yourself or your instructor, helps your learning; but it may help your learning even more to explain your developing or newfound knowledge or skills to your peers, or outside audiences, or even to hypothetical outside audiences.

But we all know this, right? Because I can almost guarantee that at some point in your teaching career you have either thought to yourself or remarked to someone else that your own learning in your subject matter was deepened by having to teach it to your students. This experience seems like an almost universal one for teachers, and it is well supported by research. We learn through teaching others. Of course, teaching consists of much more than explaining things to people, as I have been arguing throughout this book. But most of the research in this area has focused on experiments in which students taught someone else through explanation, and I think asking students to explain their learning to someone else represents the most basic route to learning through teaching. By all means you can go further than this, and have students develop more robust and creative ways to teach their newly learned content to someone else, but to keep this chapter within the realm of small teaching, I will focus on activities you can build into class which ask your students to explain or teach what they have learned to someone: themselves, their instructor, their peers, or outside audiences.

IN THEORY

We'll begin with the research that has supported the theory of self-explanation as a learning tool, and then expand into the research on the learning power of explaining to others.

The first study to demonstrate that self-explanations can support learning did so in an effort to analyze how students learned from worked examples—in other words, from sample problems that had been worked out in advance and then were reviewed step by step for the benefit of the students (Chi, Bassok, Lewis, Reimann, and Glaser 1989). The experiment consisted of two phases: a first one in which the subjects studied a series of worked-out examples from a physics textbook and answered questions to test their declarative knowledge; and a second phase in which they were asked to solve problems based on that knowledge. In this experiment the researchers did not so much prompt self-explanation as listen for it; they wanted to see if differences in understanding and problem solving would be tied to spontaneous self-explanations generated by the learners. The subject size was small, just 10 students, who were ultimately divided into 2 groups: *Good* and *Poor*. The Good students had a mean success rate of 82% on the problems, whereas the Poor students came in at 46%. The difference in the amount of self-explanations generated by the two groups is startling: Good students offered around 140 lines of self-explanation in the transcripts, whereas Poor students generated only around 20 lines. Not wanting to rely simply on volume of words, though, the researchers looked more carefully at the self-explanation transcripts and eliminated less relevant comments to tabulate only those that connected to the major ideas of the subject matter. The differences narrowed, but remained quite strong: 51 for the Good students versus 18 for the Poor students (pp. 158–159). The really interesting point about these results is that the first phase of the study showed almost no differences between the Good and Poor students in terms of their declarative knowledge of the physics principles in question. In other words, all students could score equally well when they were asked to do things like provide definitions; the stark differences between the two only emerged when they had to apply their declarative knowledge to solving problems. Robust self-explanations correlated more with conceptual learning than they did with the memorization of content.

Ultimately, the authors of this study concluded that "self explanations not only construct better problem-solving procedures, but they also help students to understand the underlying principles more completely" (p. 169). This study was incomplete in that it relied on the students to generate those self-explanations, which would have limited use for us as instructors. Obviously, we could advise students to engage in self-explanations while they are studying examples in their textbooks, but we advise students to do lots of things, many of which they ignore. The question then arises as to whether self-explanations generated in response to prompts from a teacher would have the same effect as self-explanations spontaneously generated by the students. It may certainly be the case, after all, that self-explanations worked for the Good students in Chi et al.'s initial study because those Good students were good students and self-explanation was simply one of a package of activities in which they engaged that helped them learn. However, if you isolate the single activity of self-explanation and require students of all levels to employ it in their learning activities, will it still have the same powerful effect that it had in this original study?

This was the question that Chi and another set of colleagues asked and answered in an experiment with a different group of students, this time shifting the content from problem solving in physics to understanding the circulatory system in the human body (Chi, DeLeeuw, Chiu, and LaVancher 1994). In the study, eighth graders were asked to read brief passages from a high school biology textbook about the human circulatory system and were prompted to self-explain what they were learning after each sentence they read. A second group of eighth graders were asked to read the same passages from the textbook twice but without self-explanation prompts. (This second reading ensured that they spent equal amounts of time on the text as the self-explaining students.) The students who were prompted to self-explain did so in three ways: they were instructed in advance to self-explain after they read each of the 101 sentences of the passage; every few sentences they were prompted to answer a question about the *function* of the circulatory system part they were learning about (i.e., what is the function of the septum?); they were occasionally asked by the researchers to clarify or elaborate on their initial self-explanations. Both sets of students were given pretests on the circulatory system and then tested a week after their study sessions. In these final tests, students were asked multiple types of questions about the material they read: some required memorization of basic information about the circulatory system (i.e., "What does hemoglobin transport?"), and others required them to make inferences about the system based on what they had learned ("Why doesn't the pulmonary vein have a valve in it?"). A final category of questions required them to make even more complex inferences about the implications of the circulatory system for human health (such as how the circulatory system would account for the effects of a poisonous snake bite). This range of questions seems to mimic what students typically find on exams in higher education, testing students on both memorization and more complex critical thinking skills (p. 448).

The study results confirm the findings of the first experiment. The self-explanation prompted students experienced a 32% gain in their knowledge of the circulatory system from the pretest to the posttest, whereas the unprompted students experienced a 22% gain (p. 453). Parsing the results a little more finely, Chi and colleagues noticed that the improvement was slightly more extensive on the more complex questions. In the third and fourth question categories, the prompted students improved 22% from pretest to posttest, whereas the unprompted students improved only 12% (p. 453). The study also looked at the volume of self-explanations offered by those in the prompted group, separating them out into high and low self-explainers. Even in this more finely tuned analysis, the differences persisted. Analyzing both self-generated drawings made by the students and their verbal explanations to see how they reflected an accurate mental model of the circulatory system, they found that the high self-explainers were much more likely to develop such an accurate model than the low self-explainers. "Eliciting self-explanations," they conclude, "clearly enhances learning and understanding of a coherent body of new knowledge, whether one compares the amount learned by the prompted and unprompted students, or whether one compares the amount learned by the high and low self-explainers" (p. 469). Good students, in other words, may naturally self-explain more than weaker students; however, we can still help those weaker students by prompting self-explanations.

Different theories have been proposed for the learning power of self-explanation. In Chapter One, we considered the notion that students come into our classes with pre-existing mental models of our subject matter, and that part of our work as teachers should involve surfacing those mental models with prediction activities that will help us understand and correct them. In a survey of much of the research that has been conducted thus far on self-explanation in education, Chi and another co-author argue that self-explanation supports this very process: "Learners can come in [to a class or new discipline] with their own ideas, or their own mental models of a concept. These mental models are typically flawed. When a learner encounters instructional material that conflicts with their existing mental models, self-explaining helps repair and revise their understanding" (Chiu and Chi 2014, p. 92). Sometimes when we encounter new information that conflicts with our existing mental models, we ignore it or we try to squash it into our existing frameworks. It's not that we make a conscious decision not to learn; we probably do this unthinkingly. The models are so deeply ingrained that we are not consciously aware of them. Self-explanation forces us to step back and see our existing model models. Once we have done so, then we can see what needs fixing, and engage in meaningful repair and revision in light of the new information we have been presented.

But what if it were possible to improve that repair and revision process by offering your explanation not just to yourself, or to a researcher sitting with you in a laboratory, but to a peer who was also trying to learn the subject matter? This was the question posed by a research team that put students in three different conditions as they learned Darwin's theory of natural selection (Coleman, Brown, and Rivkin 1997). One group was told to study a textbook explanation of the theory and then explain it to a peer afterward (peer-explainers); a second group was told to study the same material and then self-explain the main ideas to a researcher (self-explainers); a third and final group didn't see the textbook material at all, but listened to their peers explain it to them (hearers). After they had completed their initial exposure to the material, and explained it to the researcher or a peer, they were tested on their knowledge of natural selection and given some problems to solve. Both the self-explainers and the peer-explainers beat the hearers on the test of basic knowledge, which doesn't seem all that surprising. The more interesting difference emerged in their efforts to solve the problems, which tested both near and far transfer (near transfer problems are similar in form to the original problem; far transfer problems are different, and require more critical and creative thinking). The peer-explainers outperformed both the self-explainers and the hearers on both kinds of problems, those requiring near and far transfer. The deepest learning of the material, in other words, occurred *when the students had to explain the material to a peer*, more so than when they were just asked to self-explain their understanding to a researcher—who, in this case, was functioning as a sort of stand-in for the instructor.

Keiichi Kobayashi conducted a recent meta-analysis of more than two dozen research studies like this one on the learning power of teaching-by-explaining, and concludes that when students study or learn new material with the understanding that they will have to explain it someone else, such as a peer or outside audience, it deepens their learning (Kobayashi 2019). Logan Fiorella and Richard Mayer refined this research a little further by conducting an experiment in which they sought to determine whether students can benefit from learning something *as if they were going to teach it*, even if they don't actually teach it (Fiorella and Mayer 2013). Students in their experiment were asked to study materials on the Doppler effect in three different conditions: one group studied as if in preparation for a test (control); one group studied in preparation for teaching the material to someone else—but then did not actually undertake that teaching (preparing-to-teach); a final group studied in preparation for teaching and then actually recorded an explanatory video lecture designed to teach the material to someone else (actually-teach). All three groups were tested on their mastery of the material immediately after the experiment and then a week later. In the first test, the preparing-to-teach students and the actually-teach students outperformed the control group. But in the delayed tests, a week after the experiment concluded, the control and preparing-to-teach students were both bested by the actually-teach students. The students who had to go through the actual exercise of explaining the material to someone else, even when it was just to a camera in the form of a video lecture, significantly improved their longer-term understanding of the material.

This summary of the research, coupled with the self-explanation research, provides us with categories of activities we might develop as we ponder opportunities for our students to learn through explaining.

- Prompting students to articulate their understanding to the instructor (or to themselves) through self-explanation.
- Creating assessments in which students will develop teaching materials for someone else, such as their peers or an outside audience: slides, videos, texts, etc.
- Putting students in the actual position of having to teach something they are learning to a live audience, whether that be their peers or some other audience beyond the course.

Based on my own review of this research, my hunch is that self-explanation is probably most appropriate for newer learners, while creating teaching materials and actually teaching make most sense for experienced learners. You have to have a basic mastery of the material in order to explain it to someone else, so someone who is just getting their feet wet with it probably should not be actually teaching someone else. It would not have made sense for me to ask my daughter to teach her younger siblings to drive while she was still mastering the basics of the road. Self-explanation made the most sense while she was doing her own initial training. But once she has acquired her license and been on the road for a while on her own, she likely would deepen her own skills as a driver by having to teach those skills to my younger children.

Which, now that I think about it, sounds like something I should have done. There would have been a lot less yelling.

MODELS

The models in this chapter begin with a suggestion for how to incorporate self-explanation into classroom practice sessions.

The subsequent three models then invite you to try activities or assessments in which students will create teaching materials or offer their teaching explanations to other people, either their fellow students or audiences beyond the classroom.

Why Are You Doing That?

As we saw in the previous chapter, giving students brief periods of time in class to practice the skills they will need for their papers or projects constitutes one highly recommended small teaching strategy. One helpful thing that we can always do during those practice sessions is remind students to use the theories and principles they have learned while they are practicing. I have seen too many times that students seemed to understand a writing principle I have taught them, but then when they sat down to write their essays, they forgot about it and went back to their old habits. Providing timely reminders about learned principles and theories, and gentle nudges to apply them in practice, are great ways to prompt effective self-explanations.

Assume your students have a paper due in three weeks that requires them to make use of four or five specific writing or analytic skills you have worked on in class. You might allow the final 10–15 minutes of one class per week for students to do some drafting of those essays, informed by the lessons of that specific class period and focused on a specific step in the paper-writing process. One such brief session might be reserved, for example, for drafting an opening paragraph designed to grab the attention of the reader and entice her to keep reading. While the students complete this work, you can walk around and prompt individual students with some form of a very simple question: "Why are you doing that?" Or more specifically: "What introduction-writing principle are you using here? Playing on the reader's emotions? Surprising the reader with a shocking statistic? Seeking to find common ground with the reader?" Asking the student to pause and articulate the reason for her writing choices should help tap into the learning power of self-explanation. This general approach—pausing students who are working and prompting them to explain the principle or reason for a choice they are making—could help any time students are working in class, but it seems to me like it would be particularly helpful when students are moving toward paper or project assignments. The simple small teaching strategy here consists of pausing working students now and again to ask them to link their practice to principles.

You could just as easily require this of students who are completing projects online. For example, say you are asking students to put together a presentation for an online course you are teaching. Assume as well that you have taught them a few things about how to give presentations, such as how to combine text and graphics in ways that are visually appealing or how to ensure that slides are not overly busy with text or are clearly organized. Instead of simply asking the students to turn in the final presentation, ask them to select any three slides and write an explanation for their design choice in the notes section of those slides. What strategy for creating effective presentations did you use, you might ask them, in constructing and organizing these specific slides? Again, the hope here would be that the students who have to articulate their design strategy for three slides will learn to think about and apply that design strategy to all of the slides they are creating.

One important benefit of asking students to self-explain while practicing is that it gives you greater insight into the thought process of your students, which should help you continue to improve your teaching. Nursing educators frequently ask students to engage in "think-aloud" exercises when they are attempting to make clinical diagnoses—a consummate form of self-explanation (Banning 2004). For the teacher, this think-aloud approach can "provide insights into the types of question(s) that are asked, the train of thought, the ability to make connections and form bridges between core concepts and peripheral subjects, the use of prior knowledge and experiential learning to problem solve and the assessment of the challenges and difficulties encountered during reasoning" (p. 10). Instructors who teach in fields in which students are frequently working individually on developing specific skills (e.g., performing arts, mechanics of various kinds, etc.) should have frequent opportunities to make use of such think-alouds, as can teachers who are having students doing in-class experiments or laboratory work. Consider the think-aloud as another potential way to frame the activity of asking students to explain their reasoning, problem solving, or other cognitive work to help them both connect to principles and allow you both to better understand where they still need help.

Finally, you might consider students who visit you in office hours as ripe candidates for self-explanatory learning. When a student wants help with a paper or project or concept in your office hours, keep this research in mind and prompt the students to self-explain as much as possible, rather than simply reviewing the correct answers or strategies for them.

Peer Instruction

The use of peer instruction, a teaching strategy made famous by Harvard physicist Eric Mazur, offers a great opportunity to incorporate explanations into a class, especially larger lecture-style courses. More than 25 years ago, Mazur helped develop electronic polling as a teaching technology to support the process of students learning from one another in his courses. What he labeled as peer instruction process can take a variety of forms, but the basic model looks like this (Schell 2012):

1. The instructor poses or projects on the classroom screen a question that requires thinking or problem-solving skills.
2. The students take a minute or two to attempt to solve the problem or answer the question on their own and to record their answer with their phones or other personal response system technology (even colored index cards will work for this purpose). Answers are immediately visible to the instructor.
3. The students then are asked to take a few minutes to turn to a neighbor and explain their answer. Mazur asks students to find a neighbor with a different answer, which means that they can't just agree with one another quickly and be done.
4. The students then resubmit their answers, which again are immediately visible to the instructor.
5. The instructor asks a few students to provide their explanations for their answers to the whole room and provides the correct answer.

After this final step, the instructor has a variety of options available. If most of the students answered the question correctly the second time and the explanations elicited from a handful of students seem to be on target, the instructor can move forward to the next course topic. If, however, the answers from the class are mostly incorrect or the student explanations seem confused, the instructor can pause and revisit the topic that has been under review and then undertake the process again. Derek Bruff's *Teaching with Classroom Response Systems: Creating Active Learning Environments* offers an excellent guide for instructors interested in exploring this teaching format in greater depth (Bruff 2009).

Peer instruction strikes me as somewhere on the line between self-explanation and other-explanation. The students are talking to a peer, but typically they are explaining their reasoning in a more exploratory way, rather than teaching their peer. Still, adding the peer into the mix might push their learning beyond what they would gain from just explaining their reasoning to the teacher. It's worth noting that the success of peer instruction depends on the quality of questions you are asking. Ken Bain profiles Mazur's work in his book *Super Courses: The Future of Teaching and Learning* (Bain 2021), and points out that the questions developed by Mazur, which he calls ConceptTests, require students to engage in "higher-order thinking," and should not be ones that they can just "plug and chug." The questions are often drawn from everyday life and can seem very simple, as in this example: "You are looking at a fish swimming in a pond. Is it deeper than it appears, more shallow, or exactly as you see it?" When students have to explain the reasoning behind their answer to such questions, they are forced to apply learned theories or concepts to novel situations. Through peer instruction, Bain writes, Eric Mazur "created a space where people could struggle with their own understanding as they attempted to explain it to someone else, hear it from others, respond, and improve their thinking" (p. 89). If you need help getting started on developing these kinds of questions for your course, search online for "ConcepTests" and you will find plenty of examples from lots of different disciplines. And you can find plenty of step-by-step instructions for using peer instruction in your teaching by searching with that term as well.

Although people most frequently associate peer instruction with STEM disciplines, I have used it in my writing and literature courses on many occasions. I love to use peer instruction with my English composition students when we are learning how to navigate the process of conducting research online. This skill has become increasingly challenging for students with each passing year, especially because we should not rely on simple rubrics or acronyms to evaluate the quality of sources or individual pieces of information. Everything depends upon context, and how the source or piece of information will be used (a personal story from someone's blog can work great in an introductory or concluding paragraph, for example, but wouldn't serve well as body-paragraph support for an argumentative claim). While we are learning these skills, I put the students in pairs, throw a source up onto the screen at the front of the room, and ask them to respond to an electronic poll about whether that source offers reliable information they could use in their research papers. Then I set them loose on their laptops to explore the source in more depth, and ask them to explain their reasoning to one another. After a few minutes I invite them to respond to the poll a second time, to see if anyone has changed their mind, and then we talk about the source together as a class. This model of peer instruction has made the challenging task of teaching students about sources a much more engaging and interesting one for me—and, I hope, a more effective learning experience for my students.

Creating Teaching Materials

Recently I have been experimenting with a new assignment that requires students to teach one another by creating materials that become part of our course content. Just as we often do with presentations, I use this assignment to invite groups of students to study a course topic in greater depth than their peers, and then share their learning with everyone in the course. But in this assignment, instead of standing up and presenting their research during class, the students collect and annotate the resources they have discovered and post them to the course learning management system. In a recent literature survey course, for example, each student group had to collect the following resources for their peers on a specific topic: 2–3 accessible articles, 1–2 images, and 1 video. They needed five total sources, and for each source they had to write a one-paragraph annotation explaining to their peers what they could learn from that source. They also had to write two questions about their collections that could be used on a course exam. This was a challenging part of the assignment, as it took a little work for me to help them understand how to pitch an exam question at the right level for their peers. Finally, they had to write a concluding paragraph in which they linked the resource collection to one of the works of literature we had to read in class. Helping students understand how to complete this assignment was somewhat time consuming—I asked each group to first identify 7–10 potential resources, review them with me during office hours, and then use my feedback to winnow them down to the 5 resources they wanted to show to their classmates. I did ask each student group to finish this assignment by previewing their collections in class in a 2–3 minute presentation, but this was highly informal and ungraded. My evaluation focused solely on the quality of their resources and their annotations. I should note that as with many effective teaching strategies we devise, this one had an unexpected benefit for me; it exposed me to a wealth of new articles, images, and videos that I can use with future students.

The specific parameters of that assignment might not make sense to you, but think of all of the teaching materials that you develop for students over the course of the semester. These might include annotated resources, presentation slides, outlines or overviews of textbook readings, live or recorded lectures, handouts of various kinds, guided reading questions, written summaries of complex issues, and more. Expand your thinking even further by considering all of the sources by which people learn today: social media posts, short videos, podcasts, websites, listicles, and more. Any of these genres could become an avenue in which you ask students to create teaching materials and explain course content to one another. Our learning management systems can work very well as repositories for these materials. Of course, traditional student presentations to the class serve this purpose, but get creative and think beyond the traditional format: How *else* could your students create educational materials that would teach one another about essential course content?

Expanding Audiences

Those last examples move us into the final and perhaps most powerful method of using explanation for learning: inviting your students to teach other people what they have learned—not just you, in the form of self-explanations, and not just their peers through peer instruction or resource collections. Although this might sound like an intimidating teaching strategy to develop, it can simplify the challenge if you think about what you are doing as creating new *audiences* to whom your students can explain what they have learned, or are still learning. For the most part, students in higher education teach to an audience of one, as my colleague Carl Keyes likes to point out (Lang, *Distracted*, 2020). Students in my courses write their papers to me, complete their exams for me to evaluate, and even when they are giving presentations I find they are almost always talking directly to me, rather than attempting to present to the other students in the room. But if we want them to use the ultimate power of explanation to support and enhance their learning, then we can expand the audience for their work into new territories.

Carl Keyes provides a really outstanding example of what this looks like through his Adverts 250 Project. As a part of his own scholarly work as a historian of colonial America, Carl runs a website to which he posts every day—yes, every day—an advertisement from a colonial newspaper that appeared exactly 250 years ago to the day. Accompanying each advertisement is a brief analysis of the advertisement and its content, normally written by Carl. But Carl has folded this project into his pedagogy, and when he teaches certain courses his students take over as guest curators: they are responsible for identifying the ads, doing the research, and writing the analysis of that day's ad. Strikingly, Carl does not limit this work to upper-level students; even the students in some of his lower-level survey courses participate in this project. When he asks his students to write the brief essays analyzing the daily advertisement, he is asking them to write to a public-facing audience, one that includes both professional historians and people generally interested in American history. They have to think about how to provide context for the advertisements that will help anyone understand the nature of the advertisement, and why we might care about it. Carl's innovative pedagogy on this project has been recognized by many academic and educational organizations.

Plenty of other teachers provide inspiration for thinking in creative new ways about audience, some of whom I have written about or profiled in other contexts. Two other teachers on my campus, psychologist Sarah Cavanagh and biologist Michele Lemons, once taught a pair of linked courses in their disciplines that had a strong focus on understanding the brain. They asked their students to give a presentation on the brain for sixth-graders at a local elementary school. My colleague Cinzia Pica-Smith has asked her student to create recorded Public Service Announcements, the kind that celebrities make on television ads, to educate the campus or the wider public about an issue they have studied in class. What elements of your discipline should the wider public have a better understanding about? More recently, I wrote about the work of a scientist on my campus, David Crowley, who asks his biology students to identify something in the course that they are passionate about, and then identify an audience they think should know more about that topic. They can pick any audience they want: their parents or siblings, their dorm mates, or even a specific group of friends. Their assignment is to create some kind of project or campaign that educates their chosen audience about their chosen topic (Lang 2020). If you look around, you are likely to find plenty of examples, even on your own campus, of people asking their students to explain their learning to external audiences.

If you want to start small, though, you can even just ask students to explain their learning to a hypothetical audience. For the first few weeks of my British literature survey course, we read poems by Romantic writers such as William Wordsworth, whose work often addressed the conflict between the natural world and an increasingly industrializing and technologizing society. I can, of course, ask my students to write a standard three-page analysis of one of his poems, but one year I tried something different. At the time plans had been announced for a new technology building on campus, which would be erected in a formerly wooded area. That year I asked my students to write a three-page letter to the college president in which they used a work of Wordsworth (or another writer from the period, some of whom wrote in praise of industry and technology) to make an argument about whether it was wise to replace these woods with a new building devoted to technology. They still had to write body paragraphs in which they analyzed the poem they had selected, but in their introductions and conclusions they had to think more creatively about framing their argument. The papers were a treat to read, and I hope helped them engage with the material more deeply as they reflected upon the impact the new building would have on their campus—and their access to new technologies.

If you are looking to put this teaching approach into practice, and not sure where to begin start small. Select or create just one assignment in which students have to explain their learning to an outside audience of some kind, whether it's real or hypothetical.

PRINCIPLES

Students can explain their learning aloud to themselves, to their instructors, to their peers, or to outside audiences. The research suggests that all of these audiences for their explanation should help deepen their learning. Follow these principles as you seek to develop explanatory activities for your students.

Point to Principles. When students are self-explaining as they learn or practice a new skill, keep pointing them to principles that should be guiding them. For me the most convincing theory about why self-explanation works is that it nudges students to connect theory with practice, or principles with concrete steps, or knowledge with doing. As students are engaging in practice sessions of any kind in your class, keep asking them questions that help them make this connection: What principle/theory are you applying here? How does what you are doing connect to what we discussed earlier in class today?

Utilize Peer Power. Give students opportunities to teach one another, whether that means explaining their reasoning to a peer or creating materials that other students will learn from. When Eric Mazur asks his students to turn to a peer, he doesn't have them select their partner randomly; they are actually supposed to find a peer who has given a different answer than the one they gave. This puts increased demand on the explanation they are giving to a peer: How do I explain my thinking to someone who doesn't seem to have the same understanding that I do? That same question will apply to students who are having to create teaching materials about aspects of the course material they have studied in more depth than their peers.

Think Audience. The quickest route to the generation of explanatory activities for your students is to move them beyond the audience of one. Start small: select one assignment or activity that students usually direct to you, and direct it to a different audience. That audience can be hypothetical or real, it can be one person or the general public, it can be their peers or their parents or the president of your institution. Help them think through what that audience would need to understand your course material, and how they will have to organize and present it make an effective explanation.

SMALL TEACHING QUICK TIPS: EXPLAINING

The strategies in this chapter lend themselves both to quick implementation in the classroom and to more extensive activities that you might create for students through audience-based assessments. Start small with self-explanatory activities in class and build up to audience-expanding assessments.

- Allow class time for students to practice the skills they will need to succeed in assessed activities (as outlined in the previous chapter) and circulate and prompt self-explanations individually while they work.
- Use peer instruction with personal response systems and three key steps: students provide an answer, pause and explain it to their neighbors, and then revise their answers.
- Have students create teaching materials for their peers on essential course topics. Think beyond the traditional presentation: What else could they create?

- Invite students to direct one of their major assessments to another audience. You can pick that audience for them or let them identify an audience to whom they would like to teach some aspect of your course content.

CONCLUSION

While I was working on the second edition of this book I had a vivid reminder of the power of learning through explanation. A few years ago, I began collaborating occasionally with the Center for Teaching and Learning at Central European University, providing workshops or short courses on pedagogy for their graduate students who were considering teaching careers. In the spring of 2021, I taught a virtual four-week seminar on teaching by discussion. This was a subject near and dear to my heart. What got me interested in higher education pedagogy over two decades ago was a short article by the historian Peter Frederick called "The Dreaded Discussion: Ten Ways to Start." When I first encountered this article, I was teaching as a graduate student, floundering around in discussion sections and looking for help. I still remember what an astonishing discovery it was to realize that I could do things other than just ask questions and see if I could get anyone to respond. From that day discussion has played a central role in my teaching; nothing gives me more satisfaction than leading a great discussion about a work of literature.

I continue to read articles and books about discussion, but I am always doing so as a practitioner—I want to get new techniques I can use in my class. As I read back through my favorite texts on discussion in preparation for my seminar at Central European University, I realized that I had to take a different approach. I wasn't going to spend four weeks providing a menu of discussion teaching tricks. I needed to think more about the theoretical underpinnings for the strategies I wanted to recommend. I had to remind myself of the reasons we teach by discussion; what are we hoping to accomplish? I had to think categorically about the different types of discussions we can have in the classroom, and the different purposes they served. Doing all this preparation for the seminar forced me to re-think the use of discussion in my own teaching. I realized I had been routinely using certain strategies over and over again without really considering how they supported the larger purpose of discussion in my courses. I abandoned some things that I had been doing unthinkingly and picked up some new strategies. The process of thinking through the underpinnings of discussion, which I did in service to the seminar students, ultimately improved my work as a discussion leader.

Much of this impact, I noticed, happened during the preparatory process—both as I was doing the initial reading and as I was preparing my presentations and teaching activities. That confirmed for me the findings that learning-to-teach or preparing teaching materials can have a positive learning impact, even if we don't actually teach it to someone else. But my learning was intensified when I actually presented the material to the students, heard their responses and questions and arguments, and had to keep thinking as a result. Of course, that's ultimately what we want for students, so take that final step when you can. But ultimately the research on explanation gives us plenty of options—from self-explanation to preparing-to-teach, from preparing teaching materials to actually teaching—and they all should add a new layer of learning for your students.

Part III

Inspiration

The final three chapters of this book stem from an acknowledgment of the fact that both learners and teachers are more than collections of neural networks, or receptacles of information, or practitioners of cognitive skills. They are fully realized human beings with emotions, histories, families, communities, and more. They need inspiration as much as, if not more than, they need knowledge and skills. Connections to the human beings around them are just as important as the connections that we foster for them in the cognitive realm. We are a social species, after all, and learning is a social process. Our earliest learning comes from observing how the humans around us behave and doing our best to imitate them. As we enter school, our learning continues at the hands of teachers, but also deepens through interactions with our peers. Classrooms are thoroughly social settings, and our connection to the people around us—or lack of connection—can have a significant impact on the quality of our learning. When we feel comfortable and connected, we have plenty of brain space to devote to learning; when we feel isolated or threatened, valuable cognitive resources are being drained away in response to those feelings, and we will not learn as deeply or effectively.

In the second edition of this book, then, I have added a new chapter on belonging. When students feel as if they don't belong in our courses—because they are not smart enough, because they don't look or act like their peers, because they don't come from the same background or have the same amount of money—their learning will suffer. Their negative feelings will interfere with their learning, in the same way that fear or anxiety can interfere with a student's performance on a test or an athlete's performance in a big game. Helping students feel like they belong on campus, and in our courses, is work that faculty tend to view as outside of their purview: they see that as the work of student affairs professionals. But as more and more students are coming into higher education from non-traditional backgrounds, and as they expand the diversity on our campuses in every way, all of us need to provide our support to this essential work. Faculty can play a crucial role in helping students believe that they belong at our institutions, on our campuses, in our courses. We can help instill that belief, that sense of belonging, in many small ways which we will consider in Chapter Seven.

Emotions like isolation and anxiety can interfere with student learning, but emotions can also play a positive role in the work we do. We should think not just about how to drive out negative emotions, but also how we can engage the positive emotions that support learning: curiosity, wonder, purpose, and even joy. Emotions have a deep connection to learning, as I will argue in Chapter Eight. When we are emotionally aroused, our attention is heightened and our cognitive capacities enhanced. We are more likely to remember highly emotional experiences than we are to remember emotionally neutral ones. Instructors can be deliberate about stirring up positive emotions in the classroom and orienting them toward learning, and it doesn't take as much work as you might expect. A few minutes at the beginning of class inviting students to gaze in wonder at an image from your discipline, or listen to a story that will provoke their curiosity, can make all the difference in the world. As George Orwell once wrote, "The energy that actually shapes the world springs from emotions" (Orwell 1968, p. 141). That energy can enhance student learning in your classroom, even when you only evoke it through small teaching strategies.

The final chapter of this book arises from the conviction that teachers, over the course of a long career, also need inspiration. Just as we want students to adopt a positive and flexible attitude toward their learning, so must we. You should expect that over a 20- or 30- or 40-year teaching career you will have moments when you feel stuck in a pedagogical rut. You will undoubtedly have opportunities to step back and recharge your teaching batteries occasionally, whether that comes in the form of a sabbatical or even just two or three weeks between fall and spring semester. During those times, and throughout the various stages of your career, you might want to think about pushing into new territories as a teacher. The challenge we face right now is that the number of resources available to help you down that road are growing exponentially. We are in the midst of a glorious flowering of new books, articles, websites, social media pages, and people devoted to improving teaching and learning in higher education. In Chapter Nine, I will provide you with some directions to help navigate that swelling tide, highlighting books and other resources that should keep you engaged and learning for many more years.

You might wonder, given the crucial role that motivation and attitudes can play in learning, why I have saved these chapters for the final part of the book rather than opening with them. I did so because I wanted you to see first how small teaching changes can make a big difference to student learning, and one can see that principle displayed most clearly with concrete activities like retrieval or prediction or connecting. Thinking about inspiration, and about student emotions and attitudes, might seem like we are pushing into large and amorphous realms of the teaching and learning enterprise. However, small changes can make a major difference in these areas as well. We will therefore tackle inspiration just as we have approached our previous theories, principles, and models—by thinking small.

Chapter 7

Belonging

INTRODUCTION

One of my daughters finished her secondary education and started her college career in the fall of 2020, in the midst of the COVID-19 global pandemic. Throughout both her elementary and secondary education, she had always been a diligent and successful student. She needed no reminding or haranguing about doing her homework. She worked hard at her assignments, and took pleasure in her academic successes. But in the summer months leading up to her first semester of college, as it became clear that the pandemic would make that semester an online or hybrid one, her self-confidence began to erode. Doubts surfaced about her ability to succeed in college. She had the usual concerns of a first-year student about fitting in socially and managing life on her own, and these were magnified by the fact that the social situation on campus would be severely restricted by social distancing and other measures. But for her as for most of her peers, the transition to online learning in the spring semester of her senior year of high school had been a rough one. Her teachers, like teachers everywhere, were scrambling to adjust to the new situation we all faced and doing so with mixed success. Learning in school, which had always been such a source of pleasure and satisfaction for her, had become a stilted and unfamiliar process. The typical measures that her teachers used to measure student progress and provide feedback were disrupted. The final exams and grades and rituals that would have normally served to affirm her abilities before heading off to college were shattered by the educational train wreck that was the spring of 2020.

Because of the negative experiences she had with online courses in the spring, she sought desperately for fall semester classes which had some kind of face-to-face component. She knew how to succeed in those classes, after all, as her years of K–12 education had demonstrated to her. But the pickings were slim; she ended up with three fully online courses and two hybrid ones. Every college student will harbor some doubts about their ability to succeed in their first semester, but those doubts were magnified for my daughter by the fact that it would take place in two largely unfamiliar modalities for her. Throughout her orientation weekend and first week of classes, I spent plenty of anxious hours wondering how she was faring and sending her encouraging texts and e-mails. I knew perfectly well that she was capable of succeeding in college—I just needed to convince her of this fact.

Fortunately, in her first week of classes, one of her faculty members made a small but powerful gesture that helped support me in this work. Teaching in a hybrid format, that professor was making use of the discussion board in her learning management system, to which students were supposed to post comments about the course readings every week. When the first discussion board question was posted, my diligent daughter jumped right in and posted a comment. A day or two later, the professor e-mailed the class to encourage those who hadn't already posted to make their contribution, and in that e-mail she did a very simple thing: she thanked my daughter, by name, for launching the discussion. Immediately after receiving this e-mail, my daughter sent us a text message with a screen shot of the message: "Check it out!" she wrote. "My professor gave me a shout out!" One could argue that the exclamation points in her text, and the happiness in her voice when we spoke to her later, were perhaps not fully warranted by this experience. The professor, after all, didn't even say anything complementary about what my daughter had written. All she did was mention her name and thank her for starting the discussion. But even that tiny gesture, perhaps the epitome of a small teaching strategy, sent a powerful message to my daughter. This distinguished and distanced authority figure, one of the first she encountered in her new life in college, had taken the time to acknowledge her as a person and commend her for her contribution to the class.

My daughter's life has been rich with privilege, and she knows how to do school—her parents are both educators, after all. But all of that privilege and knowledge still didn't prevent her from having doubts about whether she belonged in college. Now imagine how magnified such self-doubts might be for students who have not enjoyed her many privileges: students who have made it onto your course roster in spite of mental and physical health challenges, discrimination based on their race or gender or sexuality or class, poverty and oppression and more. These students arrive on campus, and perhaps even to each new class they take, saddled with a question that can debilitate their learning: Do I belong here? When students walk across campus, or enter their hybrid and online classrooms, with that question at the forefront of their minds, it can represent a significant barrier to their learning. If we want to prepare students to succeed on all of the learning strategies I have been promoting in the first six chapters of the book, we have to make sure we are conveying, from the beginning to the end of the semester, an essential message: you belong here.

IN THEORY

Students might not feel like they belong on a college campus for many reasons. Students of color might see very few students and professors who look like they do, and feel isolated from their white peers. International students perhaps can't find peers or mentors who understand their specific cultural histories and identities. Students with disabilities might encounter elements of the physical campus or even the classroom that subtly prevent them from gaining the access they need. Students without money find themselves shut out from opportunities their peers are embracing, such as study trips abroad or even everyday social activities. My three oldest daughters all attended institutions which were stocked with moneyed students who spoke casually about their parents' vacation homes in Aspen or Cape Cod, while my daughters were carefully conserving the money they had saved from their summer jobs. In a 2018 story about the experiences of the rural poor at elite institutions of higher education, one student coming to the University of Michigan from a tiny rural town in Michigan told an NPR reporter: "Everybody else has got the coin that I don't have . . . I'm walking down the road and I see people with Gucci or Versace" (Nadworny 2018). This sense of feeling outside of the campus community can of course have devastating effects on the social life of these students, and lead them first to isolation and unhappiness, and then to abandoning higher education altogether. In response to these forms of social exclusion, colleges and universities have taken welcome steps in recent decades to attend more carefully to creating a sense of belonging at their institutions. On my own campus we created a Vice President of Student Success whose office dedicates itself to helping students feel like they belong on campus, and in that office they are doing heroic work in welcoming students to our community and connecting them to the institution and to one another.

But the task of helping students feel like they belong in campus should fall to everyone on campus, including the faculty. We can most certainly contribute to this work by creating a strong sense of community in our classrooms, one in which we recognize students by name and provide regular opportunities for them to interact and work collaboratively in and outside of class. We can go out of our way to reach out to the student who sits quietly in class, not interacting with peers, or whom we notice always walks across campus alone. When we have advisees or students in office hours, we can ask them about their well-being, and provide encouraging words about the work they are doing. We can refer students to the office on campus that will elaborate and intensify this work. In this chapter, however, I am going to focus your attention on an area in which I think faculty have a special role to play in supporting student belonging: affirming to students that they are intellectually capable of success in our courses. As an individual faculty member, working with an individual student at any given moment in time, I can't immediately remove systemic barriers that are standing in the way of their sense of belonging on campus as a whole (even if I am working with my colleagues to address those systemic barriers, as I should be). But I can absolutely make a difference in convincing individual students in my courses that no matter what else might be happening around them, they belong in my classroom—and more than that, that my classroom would be a poorer place without their presence.

To understand how to create that sense of *cognitive belonging* in your students, we have to clarify the barriers that stand in the way of achieving it. One very prominent line of research over the past couple of decades has demonstrated that students can feel excluded from an educational environment by a surprising obstacle: their own beliefs about their intelligence. This research originated from some experiments conducted by Carol Dweck and Claudia Mueller in the late 1990s, in which they were testing whether the type of praise we give to students after they have completed a learning task influences their approach to future learning tasks (Mueller and Dweck 1998). They gave more than 100 fifth graders 4 minutes to solve 10 math problems. At the end of the four minutes, all the students were first praised for their achievement: "Wow, you did very well on these problems." Then some of the students were given additional praise of two different types (a control group received no additional praise). One group of students received some additional *ability* praise: "You must be smart at these problems." A second group was given *effort* praise: "You must have worked hard at these problems" (p. 36). After this second praise period, all the students were given 10 additional, much more difficult problems. No matter how well they did on these problems, all were told they performed "a lot worse" this time around. This was designed to give the students a setback in their learning and to test how they would respond to failure. In the final step of the experiment, the students were given a third set of 10 problems to solve, at the same level of difficulty as the first set. Dweck and Mueller used multiple measures, throughout and after the problem-solving sessions, to measure how the students thought about intelligence, learning, and their performance on the tasks.

The types of praise that the students received turned out to have wide-ranging effects on the students and their attitudes, motivation, and performance. For example, the students who had been praised for their natural abilities "enjoyed the tasks less than did the children praised for effort." More disturbingly, "children praised for intelligence were less likely to want to persist on the problems than children praised for effort" (p. 37). What helps explain findings like this is a deeper lesson that the students seemed to be learning about the nature of intelligence and about the connection between their intellectual *ability* and their *performance* on the problem sets.

> Children praised for intelligence appeared to learn that performance reflected their ability and thus attributed low performance to low ability. Children praised for hard

work, on the other hand, did not show such a marked tendency to measure their intelligence from how well they did on the problems. (p. 37)

In other words, the ability-praised students came to believe that their performance on the problem sets reflected clearly on their natural intellectual abilities. Students praised for their efforts, by contrast, believed that their performance reflected the effort they had put into the problems. This distinction has clear and profound implications. If students tie their beliefs about intelligence to particular performances, it means that they will attribute poor performance—such as a low score on an exam—to low or deficient intelligence. Rather than seeing a low exam score as the result of not enough studying, a bad day, or some other understandable reason, they will think, "I did not do a good job on this exam. I must be stupid." The students who had been praised for intelligence thought like this. The students who had been praised for their effort did not think this way. They attributed their poor performance to their lack of effort on the second set of problems and buckled down to work harder on the third set.

But perhaps the most important result from this experiment appeared when the researchers compared the scores of the two differently praised groups on the third set of problems, the ones the students received after their "poor" showing on the second set, which were of the same level of difficulty as the first set of problems they had completed. The type of praise the students received seemed to impact *even their performance* on this third set or problems: "Scores for children receiving intelligence feedback dropped an average of .92. . .Children in the effort condition, however, improved their prefailure scores by 1.21" (p. 38). Dweck and Mueller pointed out that these results are especially surprising because all three sets of 10 problems were similar in nature, differing only in level of difficulty: "These results are particularly striking because they demonstrate that the scores of children praised for intelligence decreased after failure even though their increased familiarity with the tasks should have bolstered, not weakened, their skills" (p. 38). In other words, everyone's scores should have been improving somewhat, since they were practicing multiple examples of the same problem type. That didn't happen, though, for the group praised for their intelligence; their scores dropped. It makes excellent sense to me that the praise we give to learners might impact their attitudes toward learning tasks or toward their enjoyment of those tasks. That it actually *decreased their performance* on the problems strikes me as both profound and potentially troubling for those of us who are charged with praising (or critiquing) learners for their performances on learning tasks.

This experiment, and many more like it conducted by Dweck and other colleagues, led her eventually to formulate the theory of mindsets, the most full and rich description of which she articulates in *Mindset: The New Psychology of Success* (2008). There she argues that people have either a *fixed* or *growth* mindset when it comes to their attitudes and beliefs about learning and intelligence. Individuals with a fixed mindset believe that their intelligence is a fixed, stable quantity; someone or something stamped an IQ on their forehead at birth, and they are limited to that IQ for the remainder of their lives. Individuals with a growth mindset, in contrast, believe that intelligence is malleable and can improve with hard work and effort. Perhaps they recognize that they must work within certain limitations, but they see themselves as capable of growing and improving throughout their lives. Although Dweck's early research in this area focused on how mindset influenced students in the types of learning tasks outlined above, she came to believe that it influenced people in many aspects of their lives: "*The view you adapt for yourself* profoundly affects the way you lead your life. It can determine whether you become the person you want to be and whether you accomplish the things you value"

(p. 6, italics in original). In support of this broadening of her theory, Dweck explores in the book how the debilitating effects of the fixed mindset and the positive effects of the growth mindset have influenced major figures in the world of sports and business as well as people's successes and failures in teaching, parenting, and relationships.

Research on how mindsets can influence our success or failure has been extended to college by multiple researchers. Consider, for example, a series of studies conducted by Laura Kray and Michael Haselhuhn on the mindsets of students in an MBA course on negotiating (Kray and Haselhuhn 2007). In one of their experiments, they measured students' mindsets at the beginning of the course by asking them the extent to which they agreed with statements like, "Good negotiators are born that way" or "All people can change even their most basic negotiation qualities" (p. 64). During the semester, they put pairs of students into an extremely difficult negotiating situation, one that guaranteed initial failure and required persistence and creative thinking to get beyond. As with Dweck's fifth graders, the growth–mindset students worked better in the post failure condition; they were more likely than their peers to persist through the early failures and find workable solutions. The researchers also discovered, as Dweck did with her fifth graders, that student mindset influenced learning performance more generally. At the end of the semester, they compared the students' final grades in the course with the mindset attitudes they had expressed on the first day of the semester, and found that the students with growth mindsets had significantly outperformed the fixed mind-set students on the final course grades. The students who saw negotiating skills as something capable of improvement actually did improve their negotiating skills more substantively than those who believed them to be stable. Their attitude toward learning, at least in part, expanded or limited their actual learning.

Two challenging questions should now be at the forefront of your mind: Can we change the mindsets of students? And if so, how? Research on these questions continues to emerge; in some experiments growth mindset interventions have done their intended work, and in other cases they have failed to replicate. The research remains ongoing, and the most prominent advocates for mindset theory (including Carol Dweck) have cautioned teachers and administrators not to view growth mindset work as a silver bullet. "The new motto for mindset science," according to an overview of the debate in *Scientific American*, "seems to be this: tone down the hype and hone the details" (Denworth 2019) Whether or not growth mindset interventions have their desired effect seems to depend, as with everything else in this fallen world, on context. In the coming years I expect the research will get clearer on the implications of different contexts and the ways in which different interventions can be targeted toward them.

Still, a large-scale study published in 2019 in the journal *Nature* provides perhaps the strongest evidence yet that small, carefully designed growth mind-set interventions can have a positive impact (Yeager et al. 2019). A team of researchers gave a one-hour mindset intervention to more than 6,000 high school students who had relatively lower levels of school achievement than peers at their same institution. The intervention took the form of two 20-minute educational modules, scheduled three weeks apart, that the students took during the regular school day.

The first session of the intervention covered the basic idea of a growth mindset—that an individual's intellectual abilities can be developed in response to effort, taking on challenging work, improving one's learning strategies, and asking for appropriate help. The second session invited students to deepen their understanding of this idea and its application in their lives. Notably, students were not told outright that they should work hard or employ particular study or learning strategies. Rather, effort and strategy revision were described as general behaviors through which students could develop their abilities and thereby achieve their goals.

Compared to a similar group of low-achieving students who did not receive the intervention, the students who had learned about the growth mindset experienced multiple positive effects, including the following:

- They were less likely to believe that intelligence was a fixed quantity.
- At the end of the academic year, they had higher GPAs than their control-condition peers.
- They were more likely to enroll in advanced mathematical courses at the next grade level.

Experiments like this one affirm precisely the argument that I have been making throughout this book: that small, research-based interventions *can* make a substantive difference to student learning and performance. I expect that few faculty members are going to ask their students to complete a growth-mindset intervention module in their courses, but this experiment does provide indirect evidence that education can change mindsets—even when it represents a very tiny slice of a student's experience in a course (i.e., one hour over an entire year of high school). And it provides further evidence that changing mindsets improves student learning and achievement.

The models in the first edition of this book focused this chapter entirely on how you could make small changes that would promote a growth mindset in your students. But in the years since that first edition was published, I've come to believe that the desire to change student mindsets should serve a larger goal: helping students believe that they have the tools they need to succeed. In other words, in addition to the kinds of social or emotional belonging we want to cultivate in our students, we want to promote a sense of *cognitive belonging*. When a student with a fixed mindset fails the first exam in a course, that sense of cognitive belonging will take a significant hit. *Maybe my failure on this exam means I don't have what it takes intellectually to succeed here. Maybe I don't belong.* Instilling a growth mindset in that student could repair that sense of cognitive belonging. But we should want to do more than just change their mind(set)s. We should want to equip them with the concrete tools they will need to achieve the success of which they are capable. We should want to show them that great students seek help, and provide them with clear pathways to the help they need. We should want them to recognize not only that they can improve, but that they already have accomplished much in their lives—enough that they have made it to an institution of higher education, where we are happy to learn from them as they learn from us. Finally and perhaps most meaningfully, we should want to convince them that they have something unique to contribute to the community, something that nobody else in the world can bring—and then we should provide them with concrete opportunities to make those contributions.

MODELS

The models in this chapter begin with an activity that you can use at the beginning of the semester to affirm the unique contributions students can make to your courses, and continue with small strategies that will promote cognitive belonging throughout the semester.

Value Student Assets

A few years ago, I gave some workshops at the University of Arizona, where I was hosted by mathematician Guadalupe Lozano.

During our conversations over the couple of days I spent there in the burning sun, Guadalupe introduced me to the notion of viewing our students, especially first-year students or those who might feel disconnected from higher education, from an *asset-based* perspective. As she explained in an essay she wrote on the topic for *The Conversation*, "there are two views to take with incoming students—a deficit view or an asset view. The first sees students' weaknesses: what they lack. An asset view sees their strengths: what students bring to the table in terms of their culture, identity and knowledge" (Lozano 2020). In other words, students obviously have deficits in their learning, but they also carry assets into our classrooms. They bring the knowledge and skills they have developed in their prior schooling, and that can contribute to our common learning. They bring their unique life stories and experiences, which can help provide new perspectives on familiar questions and challenges. Students from diverse cultures or countries, students from privilege and from poverty, students with mental-health challenges or who have experienced trauma—all of them have the potential to spur new learning in our courses, and all of them challenge us to be inclusive and creative in our pedagogy. But simply *viewing* students from an asset-based perspective is not enough; if we really want to put this perspective in practice, we have to create opportunities for students to share their assets with us and with one another. When we do that, we are reminding them of the academic strengths that brought them into higher education, whether those strengths are specific knowledge and skills or unique talents or even just drive and persistence. When we ask them to tell us about and put their assets to use, we are giving them concrete opportunities to remind *themselves* that they belong here.

On the first day of the semester following my conversations with Guadalupe, I opened my class by handing out index cards and asked students to respond to the usual suite of getting-to-know-you questions: name, hometown, major. But then I explained that I wanted them to turn the card over and write me a short paragraph in response to one final prompt:

> What are you good at in school? What do you care about in terms of academics? Do you love to participate in class? Are you a good leader on group projects? This is an English class, but maybe your strength is with statistics or math. If so, tell me about it. If I know about what you're good at, maybe we can find a way for you to use it in this course.

As I flipped through those notecards after class, I was floored by the pride they took in their academic accomplishments and talents—I felt like I knew something important about each of them, and I was excited to begin working with them. I learned how hard they worked at their studies, how smartly they scheduled their homework time, how carefully they balanced coursework with sports and extracurricular activities. I realized how proud they were of their ability to work well in groups, participate in discussions, or tutor their peers. I read with joy how many of them loved to write outside of class. When I finished reading those notecards, all I could think was: What an incredible blessing to work with such hard-working and talented students. I felt so fortunate. And that perspective brought me a wellspring of fresh enthusiasm for a course that I had taught many times before, and for students whom I might otherwise have viewed as just another group of undergraduates filling the seats.

Of course the goal of an asset-spotlighting activity like this one is to make an impact on the students, not the faculty member—even though I do think any activity that freshens my enthusiasm for the course and the students will likely have positive ripple effects on them. But remember that the research on growth mindset interventions showed a positive impact on student performance and retention as the result of just two 20-minute activities. Asking students to describe their strengths is not exactly the same as asking them to change their beliefs about intelligence, so recognize that I am extrapolating here, and cannot point to research underpinning this specific activity. But if you want to take an asset-based perspective on your students, consider opening next semester by asking students the kinds of questions that will remind them why they belong on campus:

- When it comes to school, what are you really good at? What are your academic talents?
- Do you have any specific experiences or features of your identity that might provide interesting perspectives on this course material?
- What other kinds of strengths and talents do you have that might help you succeed in this course?

Make sure you give students a formal opportunity to articulate their responses, whether that comes through writing on index cards or some other format. Some students might not want to share their strengths with everyone in the room, so I suggest that students describe their assets to you alone. That doesn't mean, though, that you can't begin the next class period by providing a general overview of what you learned from them—and letting them know how pleased and fortunate you are to have such a talented and interesting group of students in your course.

Name Good Work

The global transition to remote learning in the spring of 2020 marked the first time that I taught fully online. And in those frantic early weeks of the transition, just like many of you, I was in desperate need of resources and advice. Fortunately for me, just a few months prior to the arrival of the pandemic, *Small Teaching Online* had been published, and my author copies were sitting on my bookshelf at home. I had written the theory sections of each chapter in the book, and worked closely with Flower on the rest of the book, but this had largely been an academic exercise on my part, since I had no real experience with teaching online. In March of 2020 I pulled the book down from the shelf and read it with new and motivated eyes. I knew that one of Flower's deepest convictions about teaching online has been a belief in the value of the discussion board, so I had incorporated discussion board assignments into my revised course. When I re-read what she had to say about them, I remembered that Flower argues that we should not view discussion boards like slow cookers, which we can just set and forget. Discussion boards require our regular engagement; they need tending like gardens. I was convinced by her argument, and especially by her point that one of the best ways that we can engage with discussion boards is to surface and praise the most outstanding contributions we find there (Darby and Lang 2019, pp. 41–43).

There are good reasons to do this for learning purposes, of course, as Flower points out. She describes her method of providing a written or recorded summary of each major discussion thread which highlights the most important contributions, and argues that doing so can "reinforce the learning that happens within the module to help discern what is most relevant and what they need to retain from the lively conversation that can take place online" (p. 41). As students read through a couple of dozen discussion board posts, they are likely to have trouble identifying the essential ideas, or putting some kind of organizational framework on that mass of text or video recordings. But you can do this for them, and it doesn't take much. After each discussion thread was closed, I followed Flower's advice by recording a 3–5 minute video in which I thanked everyone for their contributions, and then shared my screen and provided a brief commentary on three or four posts that I thought were most helpful for everyone to read and think about. This was actually one of the most enjoyable experiences of the semester for me. The discussion board was a low-stakes activity that was graded solely on completion, so for each new thread I read the posts primarily with an eye toward finding the thought-provoking posts that I could surface and praise.

I also followed Flower's advice by making sure I recognized the author of these posts by name. I didn't think much about the importance of this part of the process until my daughter's experience, at which point I became even more convinced of the value not only of highlighting the great work of students in your course, but doing so by name. This seemingly small and insignificant act might be the one that sends the message of belonging that your student needs in that moment. Discussion boards and online courses are obviously not the only place where you can do this. Get yourself into the habit of naming the students who make outstanding contributions to your course work, especially to the kinds of low-stakes engagement activities that I recommend throughout this book. You probably don't want to call out the names of students who ace your exams or write perfect papers, as there you might cross into privacy issues in terms of grades. But when a group produces an outstanding worksheet for an in-class activity, thank them for it. When a student makes a great contribution to a discussion, be explicit in your response: "That's a great point, Kiara, and it can really help us see this problem in a new way." If you are hesitant for some reason to do this in front of the group, which I would understand, get in the habit of sending short e-mails to students after class. They don't have to say anything more than this: "Just back in my office and wanted to thank you for your great comment in class today; it really helped me think in a new way about the topic." When a student who has recently done something good in your class comes into your office, or even when you pass her walking across campus, start with this: "Hey, thanks for the way you helped lead your group yesterday; I really appreciated that." Any one of these small comments might ease the self-doubt of a student on the margins and give her the confidence she needs to succeed in your class, or even in college more generally.

Whenever I recommend this strategy to faculty in workshops, someone will ask me about the impact that praising individual students will have on the students who *don't* get named. (And I sincerely love to hear this question, because it reminds me how much faculty care about the welfare of all their students.) I'm not sure I have a solution to this problem for large classes, but I do for smaller ones. Create a spreadsheet roster for your class or print out a copy of your roster and keep it next to your desk. Every time you single out a student for good work, put a check next to that student's name. Over the course of the semester, in a class of 20 or 30 students, everyone will do at least one thing worth praising; be deliberate about ensuring that every student name has a check mark next to it by the end of the semester.

Provide High Structure

Students spend a lot of time in my courses engaging in writing exercises or working in groups. For a long time my practice was to give them instructions orally and then set them to work. But invariably within the first minute or two of such an activity, and often to my annoyance, I would find myself having to repeat my instructions in response to the following question: "What are we supposed to be doing again?" Geez, I would think to myself, why didn't you listen when I was explaining it the first time?

When I first encountered the work of Viji Sathy and Kelly Hogan, whose writing on inclusive teaching has become essential to my thinking about education, I reflected upon my impatience with those questions with no small sense of shame. In their excellent guide to inclusive teaching in *The Chronicle of Higher Education*, Sathy and Hogan point out that one of the most fundamental ways we can support the sense of belonging in our students is by not taking for granted that students are already experts in everything we ask them to do in class (Sathy and Hogan 2019). Students who come from backgrounds of academic privilege have seen it all and feel confident in their abilities to tackle whatever the professor throws at them. If I tell students to get in groups and undertake some complex activity, those confident students are going to circle their desks and get to it. But there are always going to be some students in my class who don't come from those backgrounds of academic privilege, and who don't have that same level of confidence in their abilities or experience in doing the kind of task I am asking of them. When I put students in groups and casually throw out some directions, and those students see their classmates jump right to it while they are floundering, those debilitating questions about themselves are going to arise: "How come everyone but me knows what to do?" When I read Sathy and Hogan's work, I realized that students might have been asking me to repeat my instructions not because they hadn't been paying attention, but because they needed more help and clarification from me about what I was asking of them.

Sathy and Hogan's solution to this problem is to recommend that we put as much structure as possible on classroom experiences like group work. They advocate for what they call *high structure*, which they believe will help all of our students, but especially will help those students who come from less-privileged backgrounds:

> More structure works for most undergraduates, without harming those who don't need it. Students come to your classroom today with different cultural backgrounds, personalities, learning differences, and confidence levels.

Their very diversity may seem overwhelming at times, but you can reach more of them by sharpening the structure of your syllabus, assignments, tests, and pedagogy. In our experience, all students appreciate and thrive from additional structure, and some benefit disproportionately.

As an example of putting more structure into your teaching, they address the exact context I describe above, when we are giving students instructions for an in-class activity of some kind: "Provide clear instructions on a screen or worksheet. We've observed many faculty members give a single oral prompt, but that leaves behind students who have hearing loss, who have learning differences, or who simply need to be reminded about the task at hand." (Faculty Members Giving a Single Oral Prompt: The Jim Lang Story.) Fortunately, I have many more years yet to teach, and am happy that I can learn from experts like Sathy and Hogan on how to continue to improve.

If you too wish to create a more inclusive teaching environment through the use of high structure, continually ask yourself the questions that Sathy and Hogan pose in the article: Who might this particular teaching method leave behind? And could higher structure include those students?

- A single oral prompt for a writing exercise could leave behind students with hearing loss or an attention disorder. *Writing the instructions on the board or putting them on a slide* gives those students the information they need.
- Putting students in groups and expecting them to work out the group dynamics on their own might leave behind that quiet and self-doubting student who won't assert herself in the face of a couple of dominant talkers. *Assigning roles in the groups, and rotating those roles throughout the semester*, makes sure every student has the opportunity to contribute to the group in different ways.

- Throwing out questions and calling on the first volunteer every time leaves out students who need a little more thinking time to process the question. *Using peer instruction* gives every student the opportunity to think about their answer, respond to a poll, and then talk through their reasoning with a peer.

All of these examples involve just a little bit of extra work by the faculty member, putting some additional structure on an engagement activity—but that extra work ensures that fewer students are left behind in the classroom, and more students feel like they belong.

I'll finish with my absolute favorite example of a small teaching strategy designed to include more students in classroom discussions, one that requires absolutely zero extra preparation or evaluation time on your part, but that has the potential to create greater engagement in your courses. On the website of the teaching center I direct, we publish occasional essays by our student fellows. A couple of years ago Kelliann Keaney, at that time a senior majoring in math and secondary education, wrote an essay in which she explained that she was often labeled as a non-participating student in her math classes (Keaney 2018). But this was not because she didn't want to participate—it was because it took her a little longer to process math problems than her peers, and her teachers always called on the first person that raised her hand. Until, that is, she took a class with my colleague Jessica de la Cruz, who had a very simple policy for class discussions: she didn't call on anyone until at least five hands were raised. This simple practice, Kelliann writes, "gave all students the opportunity to solve the problem, understand the concept, and feel confident in the answer shared with the rest of the class." A student who had previously felt left behind in her classes had suddenly been included as the result of one simple practice put in place by an inclusive instructor. As you review your own teaching practices, keep asking yourself about who might be left behind, and see whether adding just a little bit more structure through techniques like this might bring them back into the community.

Normalize Help-Seeking Behaviors

In 2017 the sociologist Sara Goldrick-Rab published a *Medium* essay in which she explained that she had recently added a short new paragraph to her course syllabus, one that invited students to reach out if they were having trouble meeting their basic needs as humans:

> Any student who faces challenges securing their food or housing and believes this may affect their performance in the course is urged to contact the Dean of Students for support. Furthermore, please notify the professor if you are comfortable in doing so. This will enable her to provide any resources that she may possess. (Goldrick-Rab 2017)

Goldrick-Rab has written extensively on the costs of higher education and the impact they have on our students, most fully in her book *Paying the Price: College Costs, Financial Aid, and the Betrayal of the American Dream*, and knows better than most of us how many of our students face these kinds of challenges. What strikes me as most important about her inclusion of this "basic needs" statement on her syllabus is a very subtle message it sends: Even if you are facing food insecurity or have no stable housing, *you still belong here.* In fact, the inclusion of such a statement implies—and could be clarified orally by the teacher—that there are plenty of students on campus who face these challenges. They don't preclude you from success in college. Further, there are avenues for you to get help. These kinds of statements on a syllabus lay the foundation for a final piece of work I think we can do to support belonging in higher education: normalizing help-seeking behaviors.

Students who struggle in college in any way—with basic needs, with accessibility, and with their learning—should of course ask for help. But those students might view asking for help precisely as an affirmation of their lack of belonging. If I see everyone else getting along just fine, and I am struggling and need to ask for help, that might convince me that I'm not in the right place. In that same NPR story I cited above about rural students at the University of Michigan, one student expressed this exact sentiment: "The idea of going to someone and asking how [something] works . . . it was almost like I felt bad for not knowing" (Nadworny 2018). One of the Deans at my college likes to tell a story about the time she advised a struggling student to visit her faculty member in office hours to get additional help. "But," the student asked, "what are we supposed to talk about for the entire hour?" This story always gets a laugh, but it illustrates the problem. I assume that students know that they should come to office hours and seek my help when they need it. But that takes for granted that a student knows what office hours actually *are*, that they are confident enough as students to come and ask for help, and that they know what will happen when they show up at my door. Not only should we not be taking these things for granted, we should be going a step further and emphasizing to students that asking for help is what successful students do. We should be normalizing help-seeking behaviors.

A statement like Goldrick-Rab's can help normalize help-seeking for basic needs, but since I am focusing on cognitive belonging in this chapter, I'll focus my recommendations there. From the first day of the semester to the last, consider how you can communicate to students the following messages: Successful students seek help, and these are the pathways to help in my course. The following practical steps would convey that message:

- Include a section prominently on your syllabus about how to find extra help in your course and review the options with them early in the semester. Describe office hours and review sessions, provide information about how they can make an appointment at the tutoring center on campus. Create a forum in the learning management system for questions about the course and urge them to contribute to it (and, of course, praise by name the first person who posts there).
- Make your first quiz grade or low-stakes grade of the semester a visit to your office hours. Everyone has to come in for two or three minutes, introduce themselves, and realize that coming to office hours is not like visiting Smaug in his lair.
- Offer to meet students outside of your office as well. I know lots of faculty members who hold at least one or two office hours per week in the campus coffee shop or the library. Now that we are all deeply familiar with Zoom and its ilk, you can also offer to meet students via video. This will make help more accessible to commuters, parents, students with disabilities, and more.
- Tell students any stories you have from your own experience about the times you struggled and asked for help.

The work of normalizing help-seeking should continue throughout the semester. Provide frequent reminders about office hours, and invite someone from the tutoring center to come give a quick pitch before your first major assessment is due.

You can, finally, enlist your students to help you in this work. One of my teaching-in-higher-education heroes is Joe Hoyle, an accounting professor at the University of Richmond whose work I have profiled both in *The Chronicle of Higher Education* and in a previous book (Lang 2013). Hoyle writes a regular blog on teaching in higher education and has won more teaching awards and accolades than I would care to count. In support of normalizing the fact that students will struggle and should ask for help, Joe asks students who have earned A's in the course to write a letter to future students outlining how they managed it (Hoyle 2012). Hoyle has compiled the best of these comments into a single document that he hands out to each fresh new crop of students. The comments that he selects are almost entirely like the one below; they emphasize the challenges the students faced, and the fact that they sought help and ultimately became successful as a result:

> DON'T GIVE UP on this class. Don't do it after the first test, after the second test, or right before the final. Just don't do it. I went into the final thinking that I had a very slim chance of making an A, but I tried my hardest to do the best that I possibly could and it paid off! And even if you feel like there is no chance you can do well, go talk with Professor Hoyle. I always left my talks with him with a drive to do better.

Consider whether your future students could use a document like this one; getting it started entails nothing more than an e-mail to the students who have earned As in your course asking for a paragraph description of how they succeeded. Most A students will relish an assignment like this. Be deliberate about the ones you highlight for the next semester's students, featuring at least a few that will normalize struggle and help-seeking.

PRINCIPLES

Emphasize Growth. Your constant goal in this area is to remind or convince students that they are capable of improvement, capable of getting smarter, capable of success in your courses. It is of course true that humans are all different, and some folks have greater academic potential than others. But everyone can improve. You don't have to tell your students that everyone is a genius, everyone can earn a perfect grade in your course, or everyone has the same potential. I have had students in class that struggled mightily with writing, and it was clear that the Pulitzer Prize was likely not in their future. But that doesn't mean they couldn't get better. Everyone who finishes my class should be at least a little smarter than they were when they entered it.

Clarify, Clarify, Clarify. Success in school requires not only being smart, but knowing how to do a bunch of things that will help you succeed. It means knowing how to *do school*. You are always going to have students who have less know-how when it comes to doing school, and those students should not suffer because they didn't have teachers for parents, or attend a well-resourced high school, or come from a family in which education was the norm. Don't take for granted that students know how things work in your class. As you are creating documents for your students, or introducing new assessments or activities, or even just talking to them informally, ask yourself the question that Sathy and Hogan pose: Am I leaving anyone behind here?

Focus. The strategies recommended in this chapter will help support belonging for all students, but some students will need your help in this area more than others. If you have limited time and energy to devote to individual students, focus your efforts on the ones who need it the most. Those of us who have taught for a while can usually identify the students who feel excluded or are struggling in our courses, so make sure those students get priority when you are praising good work or sending out supportive e-mails.

SMALL TEACHING QUICK TIPS: BELONGING

Instilling a sense of cognitive belonging in your students can happen from the beginning to the end of the semester through strategies like these.

- Open the semester by asking your students to tell you about the assets they are bringing to the course: academic strengths and talents, experiences or cultural backgrounds that give them a unique perspective on the course content, or even just general talents of which they are proud.
- Surface and praise the excellent work of your students, especially on low-stakes assessments completed throughout the semester. Keep track of the students whose work you mention, if possible, and ensure everyone hears their name throughout the semester.
- Put high structure on the active learning strategies you use in class. Make instructions visible, assign roles in groups, solicit engagement through writing and peer instruction, and more.
- Normalize help-seeking behaviors. From the syllabus to your review sessions at the end of the semester, help students understand that the best students ask for help—that's part of what makes them great students. Clear the pathways to help options.

CONCLUSION

All of the models in this chapter have focused on helping convince students that they belong at the institution—but I want to conclude with some research that suggests it's equally important to convince *you*, dear reader, that students belong at your institution. This research returns us to the theory of mindsets, and gives us yet another reason to reject fixed mindset beliefs and practices. The researchers in this study surveyed 150 faculty members in all STEM disciplines at a research university in order to assess whether they held fixed or growth mindsets about their students (Canning, Muenks, Green, and Murphy 2019). Faculty were asked whether they agreed with statements like this one, for example: "To be honest, students have a certain amount of intelligence, and they really can't do much to change it." Some of the faculty in their survey embraced fixed mindset statements like this, while others rejected them and took a more growth-mindset view of their students. The researchers then looked at the course grades of all students in the courses of these 150 faculty members over the course of seven semesters. This gave them a huge amount of data: 15,000 individual course grades. Within that total, they identified approximately 1600 of the course grades as associated with students they refer to as "underrepresented minority students" (abbreviated to URM students) who were largely in three categories: Black, Latino/a, or Native American. Because they had this demographic data, they were able to see whether the faculty mindsets had a differing impact on the URM students than it did on the white majority students.

And you bet it did. The average grades for all students in courses taught by fixed-mindset professors were lower than the average grades in courses taught by growth-mindset professors. But the size of the gap was *doubled* for students identified as URM in the study. The authors of this study looked at many other characteristics of the faculty members to see if other aspects of their identity or experience could account for this striking finding: age, race, gender, tenure status, teaching experience. None of these other factors revealed a similar achievement gap. The negative impact of these fixed mindsets was not just limited to course grades, by the way. The researchers also looked at four semesters of course evaluations for the professors in the study, and found that students of fixed mindset professors also reported lower levels of motivation in those courses.

The authors of this paper conclude with a statement that encapsulates the idea of small teaching as well as anything else I have read. As they point out, institutions are spending huge amounts of money trying to address achievement gaps in STEM courses and increase the success of all students on our campuses.

But they may be neglecting the very simple and cost-effective strategy of convincing faculty to see their students as capable of growth:

> Millions of dollars in federal funding have been earmarked for student-centered initiatives and interventions that combat inequality in higher education and expand the STEM pipeline. Rather than putting the burden on students and rigid structural factors, our work shines a spotlight on faculty and how their beliefs relate to the underperformance of stigmatized students in their STEM classes. Investing resources in faculty mindset interventions could help professors understand the impact of their beliefs on students' motivation and performance and help them create growth mindset cultures in their classes at little to no cost. (Canning, Muenks, Green and Murphy 2019)

We obviously want and need funding for large-scale experiments and research that can help us discover new ways to support STEM education—and education in general—especially for URM students. But don't wait for massive grants to start improving the sense of belonging that students feel on your campus. As this final piece of research suggests, it turns out that perhaps the best way to convince students that they belong on campus is first to believe it yourself.

Chapter 8

Motivating

INTRODUCTION

I wrote my doctoral dissertation about the use of history in twentieth-century British novels, a topic that I still find fascinating. If you love a good work of British historical fiction, you and I would be able to sit down together over a cup of tea and have a nice long chat. But as most of us with advanced degrees know, writing a dissertation or a master's thesis can feel sometimes like trudging through a swamp: you struggle to put each foot forward, and the journey seems like it will never end. There were many times when, in spite of my love for my subject matter and for writing in general, I wanted to abandon the project and get a full-time job in a used bookstore, reading quietly at the counter and ignoring the customers with a cat purring on my lap. What kept me working was an awareness that only with my dissertation complete would I earn my Ph.D., and only with that degree in hand did I stand any chance of getting a tenure-track teaching position. And what continually drove me toward that goal was the fact my wife and I had a two-year-old daughter, and Anne was teaching at a private school in Chicago that paid her barely more than the graduate stipend I was making. We were struggling financially, in other words, and for years I had been promising my wife that one way or another I would get a job when I earned my Ph.D., even if I had to leave academia for it. In the end I completed my dissertation, and in retrospect I can see that what got me to the finish line were both my own passion for my subject matter *and* the external motivators that nudged me forward when I couldn't stand the thought of reading or writing one more word about British historical fiction.

If you browse the research literature on motivation and learning, you will find frequent reference to a contrast between two overarching types of motivation: *intrinsic* or *internal motivation* versus *extrinsic* or *instrumental motivation*. Extrinsic motivators include the rewards that the learner expects to gain from successful learning, such as prizes or accolades or praise or even grades; in my case the prospect of a job and the desire for financial stability were powerful extrinsic motivators. Intrinsic motivators are the ones that stem from our passion for the task or the material, or perhaps a recognition of the ultimate value of the work on some broader scale (e.g., their personal or spiritual development). My interest in my subject matter, and my desire to work through the question I had posed for myself in my dissertation, were intrinsic motivators. Although there were plenty of times when the writing felt like walking through a swamp, there were other times when it felt like nothing else in the world, as I would chase down an insight or run through a series of paragraphs with a thrill of pleasure and satisfaction.

One theory about student motivation argues that the best and deepest learning takes place when it is driven by intrinsic motivators—when, in other words (and put simply), the learner cares about the learning itself or the matter to be learned rather than about some reward she will receive at the end of the learning period (Deci 1996). In my view this theory represents a simplification of the full body of research on motivation, which suggests that what really drives learners are precisely what I experienced in writing my dissertation: a mix of extrinsic and intrinsic motivators. You can see this in all areas of life. Most of us know we should exercise, but what often inspires us to start working out are apps like Couch to 5K in which we set goals for ourselves, get rewarded with badges and stickers, and share our accomplishments on social media. I'm sure you love your job as a teacher, but I'm equally sure that you have days on which you would gladly chuck teaching, with all of its challenges and complexities, for some job which didn't require working with quite so many humans every day, with all of their unpredictable and mysterious behaviors. On those days you head back into the classroom, at least in part, because you have a job and it earns you the money you need to live. Likewise your students will have days when they find your subject matter fascinating, and other days on which they would rather do anything other than study and learn in your courses—and on those days extrinsic motivators can help nudge them forward until their intrinsic motivators kick in again.

Most educational systems are thoroughly soaked in extrinsic motivators, which take the form of grades and degrees. A vocal group of educational critics has been arguing in recent years that educators need to stop using grades for many reasons, one of which is the damage they can do to student motivation (Blum 2020). I don't fully agree with this argument; I see a role for grades to play in motivating students, in the same way that extrinsic motivators helped me finish my dissertation. An exhausted student on Tuesday morning at 8:30 in the morning in week thirteen of the semester likewise might need the prospect of a good grade in the course to get them through class that day. But I agree wholeheartedly with those educational critics that for too long we have relied on extrinsic motivators like grades as the primary or even exclusive source of motivation in education, and that we need to do a much better job of fostering intrinsic motivators in our students. Every student is different, and the right motivational recipe for each of them will be slightly different, but for most of them we are just dumping the same ingredient (grades) in the bowl in course after course. If we really want to inspire students to learn in our courses, we need to focus more of our attention on building up intrinsic motivators, leading them to learning with the same wellsprings of desire and interest that drove us into our disciplines and teaching careers.

Helping light such fires of intrinsic motivation in our students might seem like an unbeatable candidate for the Least Likely Subject for Small Teaching award. It sounds pretty idealistic to expect that 10-minute segments of class can suddenly infuse an 18-year-old with no interest in literature with a deep and abiding love of the British novel. But it's not as complex or ambitious as you might think, because we have a very accessible lever available to us in the classroom for priming the pump of human motivation: emotions.

IN THEORY

Sarah Cavanagh is an Associate Professor of Neuroscience and Psychology at Assumption University and the author of *The Spark of Learning: Energizing the College Classroom with the Science of Emotion*, a powerful analysis of how emotions impact learning in and outside our classrooms, especially in higher education. For her book Cavanagh surveyed a large body of research that demonstrates the incredibly important role emotions play in every aspect of our lives, including in the teaching and learning process. "Emotions are likely guiding your hand in every decision you make," she concludes,

> from which three plums to select from a basket of fruit to whether to leave your spouse ... It is not hard, then, to suppose that emotions are similarly guiding our students in every stage of their learning, from selecting which courses

to take in a given semester to how willing they are to participate in the discussion you're trying to drum up on the Tuesday before Thanksgiving. (Cavanagh 2016, p. 5)

You know this already, whether you are drawing on your experience as a learner or a teacher. You might know it from an experience in which strong emotions interfered with your ability to concentrate on a learning task or a course or even an entire semester's worth of courses. During the semester in college I met my wife, my learning definitely took a hit—there was a lot less studying and lot more moon-eyed dreaming. And you likely know it in more positive ways as well, such as when you were toiling away in the laboratory or reading in the library and had a sudden realization and became flush with the excitement and curiosity and happiness that sparked your dissertation or an article or book project or even an idea for a new course. Or you might know it in a more mixed way, when you felt stymied or frustrated or confused by something that drove you to resolve those emotions and learn something new.

Three key elements of the research on emotions and learning seem to me ripe for exploitation by college and university faculty, so we'll focus on those—although they don't by any means tell the whole story of the connections between emotions and learning. First, and most generally, emotions can help us *capture the attention of our students*. According to Cavanagh, this connection between our emotions and attention stems from the very reasons we have emotions in the first place. Emotions originally helped draw our attention to experiences that we might want to remember for survival purposes:

Emotions were selected for because they both influence motivation—driving us toward things that are good for survival and reproduction (high-calorie foods, attractive sex partners) and away from things that threaten our health or well-being (venomous spiders, rotten food)—and because they influence learning, tagging certain experiences and skills as important and thus critical to both attend to and remember. (p. 14)

As our brains were evolving, emotions directed our attention to what was important to learn and remember from the range of experiences we encountered every day. The terror we felt during an encounter with a predator hijacked and held our full attention, and as a result we remembered to avoid that particular path through the woods; likewise the pleasure experienced while eating some new fruit captured our attention and helped us better remember what that tree looked like and where we might find it again tomorrow. Our emotional brains still operate with these basic mechanisms in place: when we feel strong emotions, our attention and cognitive capacities are heightened. In the classroom, we can capture the attention of students and direct it toward learning by stirring up emotions like curiosity, wonder, joy, and more.

But one emotion in particular may play special role in motivating learning in education: *a sense of purpose, and especially self-transcendent purpose.* In 2014 a handful of researchers published a long study, wonderfully titled "Boring but Important," which explored what types of purposefulness most inspired learners to persist in learning repetitive or challenging yet essential tasks for future learning or academic success (Yeager, Henderson, Paunesku, Walton, D'Mello, Spitzer, and Duckworth 2014). The surprising result of this research was that *self-transcendent purpose* produced the strongest driver for students to persist through challenging academic tasks. Self-transcendent motivation contrasts with self-oriented motivation, which describes a desire to have a great career or enhance one's knowledge or abilities. Self-transcendent motivation describes a desire to help other people, to change the world in some positive way, to make a difference. The superior power of self-transcendent motivation appeared first in surveys of low-income high school seniors who planned to attend college the next fall: the ones who had the highest levels of self-transcendent purpose were most likely to actually enroll. However, it also appeared in experiments in which college students who were faced with the prospect of solving or studying difficult review questions before a final exam were reminded beforehand about the self-transcendent power of their learning:

> Results showed that a self-transcendent purpose for learning increased the tendency to attempt to learn deeply from tedious academic tasks. . . Students spent twice as long on their review questions when they had just written about how truly understanding the subject area could allow them to contribute to the world beyond the self, compared to controls. (p. 571)

As long as we are thinking about how to infuse our student learning with purpose, we may be getting the largest possible bang for our buck if we can help them recognize the power of their learning to make a difference to the world: in doing so we are both helping direct their attention and giving them the motivation to persist through learning challenges.

Third and finally, emotions are *social*. Borrowing a phrase from Marjorie Keller, Cavanagh calls emotions a *contagious fire*: they can be catching. Again, let personal experience be your best example here. How often, when you are home alone watching a television sitcom or comedy film, do you find yourself laughing out loud? Far less frequently, I would wager, that you find yourself laughing out loud when you are watching a comedy with a group of friends or watching a film in a theater. Humans are social animals, and we feed off each other's emotions. This is as true in the classroom as it is in the movie theater. The most concrete way this contagion has been analyzed in the classroom relates to the enthusiasm of the teacher and the effect that strong enthusiasm can have on student learning. For example, Cavanagh points to a study in which researchers measured markers of enthusiasm among teachers of secondary students in a Swiss school and found a startling correlation between those markers and the experiences of the students in the classroom: "The enthusiasm of the educators statistically predicted their students' ratings of enjoyment and perceived value in the subject matter" (Cavanagh 2016, p. 64). This latter finding represents the one to which we should pay special attention. The emotions that we demonstrate to students, especially our positive emotions connected to the subject matter we are teaching, can create a strong positive boost to student motivation.

The social connection between you and your students tells only part of the story, though. Of course, your students far outnumber you in the room, and it seems equally to be the case that students' emotions have a powerful potential to boost each other's motivation for learning. Dan Chambliss and Christopher Takacs demonstrated in their book *How College Works* (2014) the immense power that personal connections and relationships have on the total college experience for students, including the learning that takes place in the classroom. Their conclusions stem from a long-term study they conducted on students and alumni at their institution, based on a variety of measures, including interviews, surveys, and analyses of student work. One of the key areas in which they saw social relationships and community as playing an essential role was motivation: "Motivation is crucial. . . and emotional connections to others and to a community provide the strongest motivation" (p. 106). Students relay their levels of motivation through the amount of effort they put into their studying and assignments, through the ways they talk about their courses, through their classroom behaviors such as speaking (or not speaking) in class or participating in group work. As they do so, they are conveying emotional signals—this subject matters to me; I am enjoying this discussion; this professor is boring me—that their fellow students will catch and respond to. I've learned from my own experience as a teacher that a few engaged and highly motivated students can energize an entire class; a few students openly displaying signs of boredom or frustration can likewise derail one. Both faculty and students play a crucial role in creating and determining the motivational power of that social process.

At this point you might be wondering whether I am going to recommend hand holding or group sing-alongs to create the best emotional climate in your classroom for learning. Don't worry—I'm not a group hand holding kind of person, and I won't recommend here (or anywhere in this book) strategies that I wouldn't be willing to try myself or that I haven't tried already. The models that follow, in fact, might not strike you as connected to emotion and motivation in obvious ways; I hope they will strike you as sensible teaching practices that might fit into your classroom even if you want to avoid thinking about the emotions of your students. These six models are designed to provide the kind of positive, activating emotional boost your students need to push through the daily and weekly challenges of your courses—and they just may inspire some of them into the kind of deep and lifelong engagement that all teachers dream about for their students.

MODELS

The following models argue both for emotions that you can activate in your students, such as curiosity and purpose, and ones that you can activate in yourself, such as enthusiasm and compassion.

All of them should help provide a motivational push toward better learning.

Open with Wonder

Peter Newbury is an astronomer and the author of a wonderful little essay entitled "You Don't Have to Wait for the Clock to Strike to Start Teaching," in which he describes an activity that leverages the minutes before class start to evoke wonder and curiosity in his students. Drawing inspiration from the "Astronomy Picture of the Day," a NASA website that posts a new and fascinating image from the cosmos every day, he suggests that instructors begin classes—even before class officially begins—by posting an image on the screen at the front of the room and asking two questions about it: What do you notice? What do you wonder? He lets the image direct the informal conversations or reflections of the students prior to the start of class, and then uses it to guide a brief discussion during the opening minutes of class. Newbury suggests that this strategy can help accomplish multiple objectives, many of which have been covered in other chapters in this book. For example, such an activity can activate students' prior knowledge, thereby helping them form connections with what they already know; it also offers wonderful opportunities for learning activities such as prediction and retrieval. Obviously you could substitute anything for the NASA picture of the day: a great sentence in a writing class; a newspaper headline in a political science class; an audio clip for a music class; or a physical object in an archeology class.

What this small teaching technique really strikes me as accomplishing is a message from the instructor that hits on several of the motivational emotions we have considered already: I find this stuff fascinating, and I think you will too. Let's wonder together about it. I can't think of a better way to begin (or pre-begin) a learning experience with your students.

Open with Stories

Once class has started, the simplest way to tap the emotions of your students is to use the method that every great orator, comedian, emcee, and preacher knows: begin with a story. Human beings are storytelling and story-loving animals. As cognitive psychologist Daniel Willingham puts it, "The human mind seems exquisitely tuned to understand and remember stories—so much so that psychologists sometimes refer to stories as 'psychologically privileged,' meaning that they are treated differently in memory than other types of material" (Willingham 2014, pp. 66–67). Willingham points to the results of experiments demonstrating that people seem to find stories as having a special power to capture and maintain interest: "Reading researchers have conducted experiments in which people read lots of different types of materials and rate each for how interesting it is. Stories are consistently rated as more interesting than other formats (for example, expository prose) even if the same information is presented" (p. 68). Willingham and other researchers posit a number of different possible reasons for this, but one clear reason to me seems to be that the best stories invoke emotions. Stories have the power to induce laughter, sorrow, puzzlement, and anger. Indeed, I would be hard-pressed to think of a great story that did not produce emotions of some kind. We learned from Sarah Cavanagh that when emotions are present, our cognitive capacities can heighten; so if we can open class by capturing the attention of our students and activating their emotions with a story, we are priming them to learn whatever comes next.

You probably have plenty of stories you tell during your lectures or discussions. Perhaps you tell the stories of how certain key discoveries were made in your discipline; perhaps you tell stories about the famous people who have been major thinkers in your field; perhaps you tell stories about experiences you have had that connect to your course topics; perhaps you tell stories about things that you encounter in your daily reading, or in the news, or in movies or television shows you love. All these stories might appear in random points throughout your course, or perhaps you use them to illustrate certain key ideas when they crop up throughout the class period. The small teaching recommendation here is simply to be more deliberate about your use of stories. Take your best story and open with it. Ideally, you should use an opening story that will help pique the interest of your students in the material to come in that class period, in addition to activating an emotion or two. For example, on the day that I introduce Romantic literature in my British literature survey course, I have historically given a lecture about the economic disparities that existed during that time and that drove many writers to focus their writing on the poor and outcast members of society. This lecture went about as well as most of my lectures go—meh—until I discovered in my own reading a heart-wrenching newspaper story from that time period of a child chimney sweep who was beaten to death by his master, his cries echoing through the streets of London. My lecture on the economics of the Romantic period now opens with two stories: the tale of this poor chimney sweep and the tale of the coronation party of the prince regent, which was one of the most lavish affairs ever held in England at that time. These two stories, first individually and then taken together, help draw the students in and set them up for the statistics on wealth and income inequality that will follow. At the end of the semester, on the final essay exam for the course, I find that students still will remember the story of that chimney sweep and the spendthrift prince regent and will use them in their answers on the literature of the Romantic period.

Another way of thinking about the use of stories in your class would be to follow a suggestion made by Willingham and frame a class as a story: "Organizing a lesson plan like a story is an effective way to help students comprehend and remember" (p. 67). For example, you might open class with the first half of a story, one that should leave your students puzzled and wondering what comes next. Then launch into the class, explaining that they will now need some information or ideas or theories to better understand how to resolve that puzzle. At the close of class, finish the story. Another way to think about this would be to open the class with a question, one that the class period will help the students answer. As Willingham writes, "The material I want students to learn is actually the answer to a question. *On its own the answer is almost never interesting.* But if you know the question, the answer may be quite interesting" (p. 75; italics in original). In sum, consider how you can use the opening and closing minutes of class to set students up with a fascinating question or story opener that gets resolved by the end of the class period. The bulk of what you do within the class might change very little in this model; what changes is the frame, which you tweak in classic small teaching fashion.

Invoke Purpose—Especially Self-Transcendent Purpose

Over the course of a semester, students—perhaps like instructors—are going to occasionally lose sight of the bigger picture. When they are dug in and working on a specific and thorny problem-solving exercise during the seventh week of the term, they may forget that you are ultimately teaching them skills that will help them pass the CPA exam or will enable them to become successful entrepreneurs, or will provide them with the skills they need to end world hunger. Students need regular invocations of the larger purpose of individual exercises, class periods, and course units. The authors of a large-scale study of motivation among West Point cadets both during college and throughout their army careers argue that regular invocations of purpose are essential to creating a climate that fosters and rewards deep, intrinsic motivation. Although they use language appropriate to business organizations, the findings translate easily into education:

> If organizations do little or nothing to emphasize their purposes, aside—for example—from earning profits, internal motives may wither while instrumental motives become ascendant. Small but regular reminders of organizational purpose can keep internal motives dominant. . . a range of meaningful consequences should be highlighted (e.g., impact on others, mastery). (Wrzesniewski 2014)

As we saw from the "Boring but Important" study (Yeager, Henderson, Paunesku, Walton, D'Mellow, Spitzer, and Duckworth 2014), the meaningful consequences that may prove most effective for your students are those that emphasize the power of your discipline to help their fellow human beings or to make a positive impact on the world in some way. You will have to begin the process of motivating students in this way by reminding yourself of the reasons that your discipline does matter—something we can lose sight of after years of teaching or in the long slog of the semester. In the middle of a composition course, I'm not always thinking about the fact that powerful pieces of writing or oratory have turned the tide against slavery, have created new nations, or have inspired people to drop everything and dedicate their lives to the poor. However, I know these things are true, and they have inspired me. They can do the same for my students.

When the authors of the West Point study spoke of small but regular reminders that invoke purpose, they were speaking the language of small teaching. Such reminders about the larger purpose of your course can and should appear in any of the following ways:

- *On your syllabus.* Tune the language of your course description to the promises that your course makes to them rather than to the subject material that you will be covering. What skills will students develop that will enable them to make a difference in the world? What purpose will the learning they have done serve in their lives, their futures, their careers? Invoke this language from the first day of the course.

- *On individual assignments.* Draw from that syllabus language in every assignment. Use words and phrases that tie each assignment at least one step up toward your course promises: "This paper assignment is designed to help you develop your skills in crafting a thesis and using evidence to support an argument...These presentations should prepare you to make effective sales pitches to organizations or groups..."
- *On the board, real or virtual.* The simplest way to connect individual class periods to the course purpose is to keep that connection in front of their face during class, real or virtual. Have a simple but overarching course or unit outline that you can write on the board each class period, and then note exactly where this class falls within that larger picture. This could be done on the actual board or on your course website's individual pages.
- *In the opening and closing minutes of class.* Use those coveted time periods to remind students where they have been, where you are now, where you are going, and—most important—*why.*

As long as you have made your initial case about the purpose of your course effectively, on your syllabus and in the opening weeks of the semester, you should need only small reminders to help students reconnect to that purpose throughout the term.

Share Your Enthusiasm

If you want students to care about the material, you not only have to care about it yourself—which I will take for granted that you do—but you also have to *demonstrate to them* that you care about it.

You can find lots and lots of research in the educational literature on the role that teacher enthusiasm plays in inspiring students to learn, and you can find plenty of grumpy responses from instructors who claim that they should not have to dance around and sing the praises of the material to inspire student learning. At one point in my career, I remember reading a bunch of the literature on this subject and having this same grumpy reaction, which stemmed from my more introverted leanings. At that time I was teaching an upper-level seminar on British literature, and the students were participating very well in our class discussions. They didn't need my enthusiasm or inspiration anymore, I reasoned. So I prepared very thoroughly for the next class but decided that I was not going to do what I normally did at that time—namely, sweeping into the classroom with lots of energy and attempting to spark their discussions with my own enthusiasm for the book we were reading. I came into class that day and sat down in the midst of the students at the long table in our seminar room, without any preliminary inspirational opening, and spoke very quietly about the book we were reading for a few minutes. Then I attempted to start a conversation. In 20 years of teaching, that class was the worst class I have ever experienced. Even though I have probably taught thousands of individual class sessions, I still remember vividly not only the horrible feeling of being in that lifeless classroom, but also the profound sense I felt afterward of being *so completely wrong*. I realized at that moment that no matter how great my students are or how well the class is going, I still have to inject some of the energy into the room. To put it in the terms of Sarah Cavanagh's book, for a contagious fire to alight in my classroom, I have to start the process by striking the match.

With that said, you still don't need to dance around and sing to demonstrate to your students that you care about this material, that it matters to some larger context (their lives, their community, the world), and that you want it to matter to them. You can do this with occasional asides in class about the moments in your own learning that really sparked your interest or led you toward some exciting new discovery. Or you can do it by noting when the course arrives at the material that you find most interesting or important: Of all the books we are reading this semester, this one's my absolute favorite—I've read it 20 times and still find new insights in it; this particular problem never fails to fascinate me; I have been waiting all semester to get to this point because now we are facing the most intriguing challenge that most of you will confront in your careers. The small teaching recommendation here simply involves allowing the enthusiasm that you felt when you were first studying your discipline—or that you show to your peers and colleagues when you are talking about your favorite features of your discipline—show in your classroom as well. The personality that appears when I am talking to a colleague in the hallway about the most recent book from my favorite novelist should find its way into my classroom.

That can happen in lots of small ways; it takes only a deliberate decision to open that side of yourself to your students in as many class periods as possible. You'll have your dull and uninspiring days, as we all do. But I once heard a recommendation that has helped me tap into that enthusiasm more effectively. I wish I could remember and credit the individual who told me this, but it occurred at one of the many teaching conferences or workshops I have attended, and the details are lost in the recesses of my memory. What I do remember is this faculty member explaining that before every class session, they sat down in their office chair for five minutes to gather their thoughts and—more importantly—to remind themselves about what they found so fascinating about their discipline. They tried to re-capture that sense of wonder they felt when they first began learning about whatever subject matter was on the agenda for that day. That's all it took for that person to inject energy and enthusiasm into the class. Even if it's only one or two minutes, experiment for a few weeks with pausing before you head over to class each day, disconnecting from your devices and just gathering your thoughts. Use those moments to connect with whatever you find most fascinating about that day's material, and let it rise to the surface of your mind—allowing it to remain there throughout class.

Pay Attention to Every Student

I had the opportunity to attend an event a few years ago on my campus in which we discussed how individual relationships with students can impact their learning. A colleague in psychology, Paula Fitzpatrick, offered the following fascinating contribution to this discussion. She was an introvert, she said, but she had decided that she wanted to make a more deliberate effort to connect with the students in her classroom. In the previous semester she had shown up to every class session 5–10 minutes early and—even though she found it a struggle—spent a few of those minutes approaching individuals in the class and engaging in casual conversation. She did so in a carefully planned way, ensuring that she approached every student at least once over the course of the semester: "Even that stony-faced kid sitting in the back row—I made sure I spoke to him too." When her student evaluations came in after the semester had ended, she was quite surprised to find that multiple students noted this simple practice of hers as something that contributed to the overall positive atmosphere in the classroom. What struck her about this particular experience that differed from previous semesters was that in the past she might have engaged in occasional patter with the students in the front row; this semester she made the effort to speak to each student individually at least once.

To help understand why this small gesture might matter so much to students and how it connects to their emotions, consider one of the more fascinating findings from Chambliss and Takacs's study reported in *How College Works* (2014). In collaboration with others at their institution, the authors analyzed a massive survey of student writing at their college, trying to determine whether student writing improved over the course of a student's four years. One surprising result of this analysis was that many students demonstrated very fast gains in writing in their first year of college—sometimes within weeks or months of arriving at the college. This happens less because of any specific instruction, they concluded, than it does for the very simple reason that instructors at the college they studied make a strong commitment to responding to student papers, both in their comments and in individual student conferences. When the students see that instructors are actually reading and critiquing their work, they become motivated to work a little harder at their writing—and that harder work pays off in some immediate gains in their writing abilities. As Chambliss and Takacs explained, "What mattered from professors was the sheer fact of paying attention: she took the time; he helped me. Attention says to the student, 'Writing matters'; but more, it says, '*Your* writing matters'" (p. 112, italics in original). This suggests that the sheer fact of paying attention to student work spurs a motivational boost. In the same way, my colleague's experience suggests that paying attention to students in class made a noticeable difference in creating a positive atmosphere in her classroom and even—as she explained to us later—increased the number of students who participated in classroom discussions.

See if you can find ways to use the periphery of the class period—those minutes before class starts, or after class starts, or outside of the strict content of your online courses—to pay attention to the individual learners in your course. Chambliss and Takacs's research suggests that this very simple act can not only boost the motivation of your students, but can even improve their learning.

Warm Up Your Language

The pandemic brought a welcome new attention to the fact that our students are human beings with vulnerable bodies and complex lives outside of our courses, and that higher education faculty in general have to do a much better job of engaging in *cura personalis,* or the care of the whole person. This Latin phrase comes from the spiritual teachings of Saint Ignatius of Loyola, and has long been a feature of Jesuit education (as I learned during my years as a student at Jesuit institutions). *Cura personalis* should become part of all of our thinking about the education we offer our students. Some of the recommendations I made in the previous chapter will contribute to that care of the whole student, but I want to finish this chapter with one final strategy that you can use to demonstrate better care for your students, creating the kinds of social connections that will encourage your students to ask for help when they need it.

Over the past few years some researchers have been looking at the difference between "warm" and "cold" language in course documents like syllabi or assignment sheets. Cold language consists of neutral descriptions of policies and consequences; warm language is empathetic, compassionate, and inviting. It explains the reasons for policies, encourages students to seek help when they need it, and conveys understanding for the challenges students face. One study conducted by Regan Gurung and Noelle Galardi (2021), asked more than two hundred students to read syllabi that were written in warm and cold tones, and then surveyed them about their willingness to reach out for help to that instructor. Students reading the warm-toned syllabi reported greater willingness to ask for help in several key areas, including when they were having problems with a class assignment. Here's an example of what a warm-toned syllabus statement related to missing or late work looked like in the experiment: "Such life events are unwelcome and because I understand how difficult these times are, . . . I will be happy to give you a make-up exam." Contrast a sentence like this with the kind of cold-toned statement that I have seen on many course syllabi: "Late work will not be accepted." Imagine yourself as a student in both of those courses: Which instructor are you going to ask for help? In which course will you see the instructors as someone who cares about you and your learning? In which course are you more likely to follow that instructor on a challenging learning journey?

When cell phones first began to make their way onto college campuses, and into our classrooms, I added a statement to my syllabus that I now recognize was ice-cold:

> PUT AWAY AND TURN OFF YOUR CELL PHONES! If your phone rings or vibrates in class, or I see you checking it or texting, you will be absent for that day.

Brrrr. Not only is there no compassion or empathy here, there are also all caps and exclamation points to drive home the inflexibility of my attitude. A dozen years later, with the research on warm-language syllabi under my belt, my policy on the use of technology in the classroom begins like this:

> We are all challenged these days by the ways in which our digital devices—including laptops, tablets, and phones—can steal our attention away from our immediate surroundings. In this class we will have a technology policy that is designed to support your attention to one another and to the course material.

And ends like this:

> If anyone has an accommodation that would make any of these policy items challenging in any way, please let me

know by e-mail prior to Wednesday's class. I will make sure I modify the policy accordingly. *I am very happy to do this*. If you have any other hesitations or concerns about the policy, for any reason at all, please let me know that as well. I want to ensure that this policy supports our work while meeting your needs as a student.

Writing this newer policy made me feel like I was working in collaboration with my students on a shared challenge, rather than acting like the prison warden laying down the rules and consequences for violators.

As your final act in support of student motivation, then, read through your syllabus before the next semester begins, and look carefully at the tone of it. Where do you see cold language? And how can you warm it up?

PRINCIPLES

Use these three basic principles to guide both your motivational strategies and your own reading on this most important of topics for teachers at any level.

Acknowledge the Emotions in the Room. They are there. You can't do anything about that. Rather than see that as a negative, instead look at the positive possibilities. You can tell stories, show film clips or images, make jokes, or do any number of things that will briefly activate the emotions of your students and prepare them to learn. You can leverage the power of emotions to heighten the cognitive capacities of your students at the opening, midway point, or closing of a course or a class period.

Show Enthusiasm. First, care about your course material. If you are not excited by what you are teaching, and if you do not care deeply about it, don't expect your students to care about it either. But they won't know that you care deeply about it unless you are willing to show that to them, however that might seem best to you. Second, care about your students' learning. That means acknowledging that they are full human beings, not cognition machines, and the noncognitive parts of them sometimes will distract them from learning tasks. Let that awareness hover in your mind as you write course materials or interact with students who are not performing as you think they should, and allow it to govern the tone of your interactions.

Evoke Purpose. We all know that the learning students do in our courses has the potential to improve their lives. A student who can produce great writing that moves audiences will be a better candidate for almost any professional career, and could also use their writing skills to have a greater impact in their chosen fields. But the pathway to that purpose from a grammar lesson on Wednesday morning in the seventh week of the semester can be a long and invisible one for students (and sometimes, frankly, for me). Think continually about the ways in which you can remind students of the ultimate purpose of their learning, first to improve their own lives—but perhaps more importantly, to make the world a better place.

SMALL TEACHING QUICK TIPS: MOTIVATING

Students bring into our courses a complex mix of backgrounds, interests, and motivations, and we can't turn every student into a passionate devotee of our discipline. We can, however, help create better learning in our courses with attention to some small, everyday motivational practices that have the power to boost positive emotions and learning.

- Open individual class or learning sessions (and even readings) by eliciting student emotions: give them something to wonder about, tell them a story, present them with a shocking fact or statistic. Capture their attention and prepare their brains for learning.
- Consider how practitioners in your field, or the skills you are teaching them, help make a positive difference in the world; remind them continually, from the opening of the course, about the possibility that their learning can do the same.
- Show enthusiasm for your discipline, for individual texts or problems or units, and for your hope that students will find them as fascinating as you do.
- Get to class early every day and spend a few minutes getting to know your students, learning about their lives and their interests, and creating a positive social atmosphere in the room.
- Warm up the language of your course documents, starting with your syllabi. Envision a student reading the course policies on your syllabus: How approachable do you seem to them? How willing are you to give them help when they need it?

CONCLUSION

Thinking about the emotions of my students, and the role that they play in their learning, is challenging for me. I have worked for many years now with Sarah Cavanagh, whose work animated the theory section of this chapter, and she once pointed out to me that when conversations with colleagues on campus take a strong emotional turn, she can see me physically shrinking into myself, as if I want to disappear. That observation is accurate; I have always found myself uncomfortable in the presence of strong emotions, and in general I am not all that attentive to emotions in myself or other people. Whenever I am in a faculty meeting and someone begins to show an emotion like anger or frustration, it takes me completely by surprise. I thought we were just having an interesting exchange of intellectual views, while apparently some emotional stew was bubbling under the surface of people's comments—and I had no sense of it whatsoever.

All of this is to say that for a long time I paid little attention to the emotions of my students—not because I didn't care about them, but because I don't pay all that much attention to emotions in general. But it's impossible to ignore the findings of the research on motivation and emotions. If we want to be effective teachers (and I do) than I have to pay at least some attention to the emotions in the classroom, both mine and my students. I have found that doing so has created a stronger sense of connection to my students, and I have welcomed that change. The more I get to know them and learn about their lives, the more I am amazed by their accomplishments, and the more invested I feel in their learning. Even if you share my discomfort with the idea of working with the emotions of your students, I can assure that even small investments of time and energy into this part of your teaching work can pay substantive dividends—both for you and for your students.

Chapter 9

Learning

INTRODUCTION

During my final year of graduate school, I was looking for a part-time job to supplement my university stipend. I had worked at a used bookstore throughout most of graduate school (it turns out that working at used bookstores entails more than sitting behind a counter with a cat on your lap), but my wife and I had moved to a new apartment and it didn't make much sense for me to commute 30 or 40 minutes a day through Chicago traffic to earn late-90s used bookstore wages. I saw an advertisement for a graduate fellow position at the Center for Teaching Excellence on campus, and it seemed like the number of hours was about right for me. I had no idea what a Center for Teaching Excellence was, but I sent in my application and got an interview. The director of the center at that time was Ken Bain, a historian whose powerful and influential works—still germinating at that time—include *What the Best College Teachers Do* and *What the Best College Students Do*, two best-selling accounts of the habits and practices of highly successful faculty and their students. Ken and I had a good conversation, and he offered me the job. My task would be to assist in the development of programs for graduate students, to help him continue the research he had been conducting for *What the Best College Teachers Do*, and to serve as a general factotum around the teaching center, assisting with whatever other projects demanded our attention. I enjoyed the work so much that when I finished my dissertation the next year, I applied for a position as assistant director, and served in that position for the next three years.

What drew me into the work of studying teaching and learning in higher education were two things that Ken did for me, one specific and one more general. The specific thing that Ken did when I was first hired was point me to the bookshelves and file cabinets in the center, all of which were stuffed with monographs and articles on teaching and learning, and say, "Take some time and explore the library. Read around a little bit in the subjects that interest you." I was teaching as a graduate student at that time and struggling to get students engaged in meaningful discussions of the literature they were reading, so I immediately pounced on the articles about teaching by discussion. From that moment on, I got into the habit of addressing any teaching problem I might have by first digging into the literature in search of research and recommendations.

But beneath this specific invitation that Ken issued to me to explore the literature, he did something much more substantive. In his approach to faculty development, in the books he wrote and the talks he gave, in everything he did in this field, he communicated to me and to his audiences a fundamental idea that has animated my career ever since: helping another human being learn is a fascinating challenge, one as worthy of our scholarly attention as are the questions we pursue in our disciplines. Strange though it might seem, this had never occurred to me before. I had always walked into the classroom wondering how I was going to teach. It never occurred to me that my actual job was to help people learn. Of course, once you make this mental shift, an avalanche of questions follows. How *do* people learn? What happens in the brain when we learn something? Why does learning fail at times and succeed at other times? Why do we forget some things we learn and remember others? What inspires people to learn, and what turns them away from learning? As in almost every scholarly field, questions like these expand and twist and multiply as you pursue them, and in my case have never stopped sending me back to the scholarship of teaching and learning in higher education, wondering how to solve the latest problem I have encountered in my classrooms.

In this final chapter, wholly reconceived for the second edition, our focus will thus turn to learning—your learning, not your students. I hope your reading of this book means that you too have an interest in the fascinating question of how to help other human beings learn, and that you intend to continue your journey as a student in this burgeoning scholarly field. And I don't use the word burgeoning lightly—the past few decades have seen an absolute explosion of new articles, books, and other resources on teaching and learning in higher education. Every author of course wants you to believe that their particular topic offers the master key for good teaching, and it's easy for anyone to get overwhelmed by the sheer volume of teaching approaches and practical tips you find in the scholarship of teaching and learning. The goal of this chapter is twofold: to acquaint you with some enduring classics in the field, and then to introduce you to some current people and resources whose work will repay your attention and produce the greatest possible dividends in your studies.

IN THEORY

I hope you don't require much convincing that you should continue to learn as a teacher—you wouldn't be reading this book if you didn't already believe that to a certain extent. Thus, I'll keep the theory section of this chapter brief, and use it to articulate the three primary reasons that have made me a lifelong devotee of the literature on teaching and learning in higher education.

First, our students are always changing. This happens at both the micro and macro level. Sometimes I am teaching two sections of the same course, in back-to-back time slots, and find that my carefully prepared teaching plans work amazingly well with one of those classes and fail miserably with the other. Each community of students has its own personality and requires continuous small adjustments to our teaching. But our students are changing throughout higher education as well, as our campuses and classrooms are opening up to an increasingly diverse student population. In addition to the growing numbers of Black and Hispanic students in higher education (U.S. Dept. of Education 2019), we are seeing more and more first-generation students, students with physical and mental health challenges, and students from across the socioeconomic spectrum (Center for First-Generation Student Success 2020; DeAngelis 2019). These are all fabulous trends that enable higher education to become a truly transformative enterprise. But these changes to our student populations mean that we have to do *the work*: we have to welcome these students to campus, build community with them, help them feel like they belong, understand the knowledge and experiences they bring to our courses, and identify the teaching strategies that will best help them build and grow from where they are now. The recommendations for inclusive teaching that I referenced in Chapter Seven represent the kind of thinking that we need to undertake continuously in light of our ever-changing student populations. The question that we have to ask ourselves each year is how we are going to teach the actual students in our courses, and not the students who were in our courses 5 or 10 years ago. That question should inspire us to continue learning.

Second, our understanding of the learning brain, like our understanding in almost every scholarly field, continues to grow and evolve. Some of the new discoveries made about the brain by neuroscientists and cognitive psychologists have clear implications for teachers. For a long time brain research and educational practice seemed to operate in two separate spheres. But especially in the past decade research on learning and the brain has been translated into accessible forms for working faculty both by scholars in the field and by synthesizers like myself. Most of the books and websites that I will recommend in the next section come from people who either have conducted their own research and experiments on learning, or who have taken a deep dive into the literature and returned with practical recommendations for faculty. I do see teaching as both an art and a craft, and the humanities part of me sometimes cringes at the seemingly *de rigueur* phrase these days that our teaching methods have to be "evidence-based." Teaching is not a mechanical process; we can't always follow evidence directly into practice in our particular contexts. We need creativity and experimentation. But we should create and experiment with at least a basic understanding of the process of human learning in mind. Since our understanding of the learning process continues to evolve—just as our understanding of almost every scholarly field continues to evolve—we should do our best to stay on top of the most important developments. The websites that I recommend in the next section, especially Retrieval Practice and the Learning Scientists, will help you stay current with the latest research on learning and its implications for teaching.

Finally, maintaining a teaching career over the course of a few decades requires regular infusions of new energy and enthusiasm for you as a teacher. I have taught English composition and Introduction to Literature dozens of times in the last 20 years. Usually after a few iterations of a course, I have a solid grasp on what works, and could ride out my basic approach for a lifetime. But doing that would gradually wear away my passion for those courses, and I have no doubt that the erosion of my passion would have ripple effects on my students. I would much rather change two or three things every semester, even if I know that one of them will fail, than continue to teach in the exact same way, because such changes keep me engaged. I'm a little more energetic, a little more curious, a little more off-balance on the days or semesters in which I am trying new things. When those new thing go well, I want to try them again; when they fail, I want to understand why. In both cases I'm learning new things about teaching, learning, and my students—and, as I expect is true for you as well, learning new things is one of the great pleasures in my life. We should therefore not apologize for making small, continuous changes to our teaching in service to our own professional satisfaction and enthusiasm. The more satisfied and enthusiastic I am as a teacher, the more I will bring my best self into the classroom, the one most likely to make a difference to the lives of my students.

The resources below are my trusted guides to making the kinds of small and ongoing changes to my teaching that have kept me energized for the past 20 years, and that I hope will keep me inspired for many years to come.

RESOURCES

My goal in providing these resources is to point you to some productive pathways for your future learning without overwhelming you. I have perhaps erred on the overwhelming side in the books category, but in the others I have limited myself to just a few essential entries. There are many more out there, but these give you good starting points.

Books

As you may well imagine from the fact that I am a writer of books, I prefer to get new information and ideas from books. The following titles include both enduring classics on higher education pedagogy and some newer titles on how people learn.

- *What the Best College Teachers Do* (Bain 2004). Ken Bain's elegantly written analysis of highly effective college teachers remains for me the first book that all college teachers, new and experienced, should read at some point during their careers. In this book you can get a taste of the experience I had in my formative years working with him at the teaching center, having my eyes opened to the fascinating problem of how to help another human being learn.
- *Make It Stick: The Science of Successful Learning* (Brown, Roediger, and McDaniel 2014). An expertly researched, and well-written book on how people learn and what it means for us as teachers (and learners). Two cognitive psychologists (Roediger and McDaniel) teamed up with a novelist (Brown) to make this book an especially readable entry in the field. The book is addressed to a general audience, not just teachers, but the implications for teachers shine through pretty clearly.
- *How Learning Works: Seven Research-Based Principles for Smart Teaching* (Ambrose, Bridges, DiPietro, Lovett, and Norman 2010). The title says it all. Aimed at college and university instructors, a clear and well-researched overview of what college teachers should know about topics like learning, motivation, feedback, and student intellectual development.
- *Why Don't Students Like School?* (Willingham 2009). Although Willingham's book articulates its audience as K–12 teachers, this college instructor found in it enough useful and fascinating information about learning and teaching to merit my highly recommending it to college and university instructors as well. A new edition of this book was published in April of 2021.
- *Teach Students How to Learn: Strategies You Can Incorporate Into Any Course to Improve Student Metacognition, Study Skills, and Motivation*

(McGuire 2015). In some future edition of this book, I'm going to get around to writing a chapter about metacognition—helping students become more aware of their own learning processes and improve them. When I write that chapter, I will most certainly draw from Saundra McGuire's excellent book, which provides plenty of concrete recommendations for helping your students become better managers of their own learning and education.

- *For White Folks Who Teach in the Hood . . . and the Rest of Y'All Too* (Emdin 2016). As with Daniel Willingham's book above, the primary audience for this book is K–12 educators, but as with Willingham, I think the analyses and recommendations of Christopher Emdin translate easily to higher education. If you want a better understanding of the life experiences and cultural backgrounds of your increasingly diverse student bodies, and new approaches for teaching them effectively, Emdin provides an excellent starting point for your learning.

- *Discussion in the College Classroom: Getting Your Students Engaged and Participating in Person and Online* (Howard 2015). Sociologist Jay Howard's book analyzes the social norms that can support of interfere with student participation in your courses. I'm not sure any book on education has more radically upended my thinking about student engagement, and given me new ways to understand the classroom, than this one.

- *Minds Online: Teaching Effectively with Technology* (Miller 2014). Although the research in this area moves quickly, cognitive psychologist Michelle Miller focuses on principles and practices that are still essential reading for anyone who teaches online or uses technology in their teaching (i.e., pretty much all of us). You'll find here recommendations on everything from the use of images in your presentation slides to the design principles that should animate your online teaching.

- *Distracted: Why Students Can't Focus and What You Can Do About It* (Lang 2020). During the years following the publication of

Small Teaching, I found myself increasingly interested in the literature on attention and the role it plays in learning—and upon the ways in which digital devices in the classroom were sometimes helping and sometimes hurting the learning of my students. In this book, I argue that instructors need to recognize the challenges to attention that our students face in their learning—and that all of us face in the digital era—and I offer my perspective on the ways in which we can best support student attention in our courses.

- *Small Teaching Online: Applying Learning Science in Online Classes* (Darby, Lang 2019). When I first started giving presentations on the material in this book, people always asked me about how to apply them online. I used to joke that I was happily accepting applications for co-authors. Flower Darby approached me after one of those presentations and offered her service. *Small Teaching Online*, largely authored by Flower with some support from me, expertly applies the concept of small teaching to the online and hybrid courses that so many of us are teaching now.

Book Series

Give someone a fish, the saying goes, and you feed that person for a day; teach them to fish and you have fed them for a lifetime. The above books are all fish that should keep you sated for at least a year's worth of reading, but eventually you'll want to catch your own dinner. The publishers below are the places to search for more titles in your areas of interest.

- *West Virginia University Press.* For the past five years I have been working with WVUP's director, Derek Krissoff, to build a new list of titles on teaching and learning in higher education. We now have ten titles published and another dozen in the pipeline. You can find in our series books from higher education heavyweights like Kevin Gannon, Sarah Cavanagh, Josh Eyler, Derek Bruff, Susan Blum, Tom Tobin, Michelle Miller, and Jessamyn Neuhaus.

- *Princeton University Press*. Former press director Peter Dougherty has been building a new list of titles called Skills for Scholars, and this series of compact books represents an impressive new entry to the field. Just a handful of titles have appeared thus far, but the books are all very high quality—and typically very concise, making for manageable reading during a busy semester.
- *Jossey-Bass*. You are holding a Jossey-Bass book in your hand, and this division of the larger publisher Wiley has long published great books for teachers. Four of the ten books in the list recommended above are Jossey-Bass titles, and you can find many more well-researched volumes in their Professional Learning series.
- *Stylus*. With the largest catalogue of books on higher education teaching and learning that I know of, Stylus has a book on just about every subject you can imagine in the field. Their enormous output means the quality can occasionally be mixed, but you can find reliably good titles in the Excellent Teacher series edited by Todd Zakrajsek.

Web Resources

When you have a teaching problem or a specific topic you want to learn more about, you probably begin with your generic search engine. You will be more likely to find resources that have been produced and vetted by leading experts in the field if you instead visit any one of the following websites and conduct your search there.

- *Vanderbilt University Center for Teaching*. The Center has done a remarkable and heroic job of creating guides to almost every imaginable aspect of teaching and learning in higher education.

The guides provide theoretical background, practical recommendations, and sources for further consideration. Simply outstanding work by director Derek Bruff and his team.

- *Carnegie Mellon University Eberly Center for Teaching Excellence and Educational Innovation.* Marsha Lovett and her colleagues at the Eberly Center have done similarly excellent and generous work in preparing an extensive set of freely available resources on teaching and learning in higher education. You can both browse through their guides or visit their "Solve a Teaching Problem" site to get immediate, directed help.

- *The Learning Scientists.* If this book has sparked your interest in the mechanics of learning, and you found yourself fascinated by the many studies I describe in the theory sections of each chapter, visit this excellent website to stay current in this area. The four women hosting the website are all early-career cognitive psychologists who highlight new research coming from the learning sciences and provide overviews and implications for teaching. On the website you can find essays, teaching guides, and a podcast. Everything is free, but they welcome (and deserve) support through Patreon.

- *RetrievalPractice.org.* Pooja Agarwal, whom you met in Chapter Two, is a cognitive psychologist whose research focuses on the powerful learning effects of retrieval practice; along with sixth-grade teacher Patrice Bain, she is the author of a book called *Powerful Teaching: Unleash the Science of Learning,* which is aimed at K–12 teachers. On this website Pooja covers much more than retrieval, and offers—in addition to overviews of research and links to other sources—teaching guides that you can download for free. As with the Learning Scientists, it's an excellent site for discovering new research on learning and its implications for teaching.

- *Inclusified.* Viji Sathy and Kelly Hogan are the authors of a forthcoming book on inclusive teaching, and their research-supported recommendations for how to make every student feel included in your courses are eminently practical—just the kind of thing that this small teacher loves. Until their work is available in book form, visit their website to learn more about their approach to inclusive teaching (or read their outstanding guide to inclusive teaching in the *Chronicle of Higher Education*: Sathy and Hogan 2019). If you have the resources, bring them to campus to offer one of their popular workshops for faculty and staff.

Podcasts

Sometimes my life feels like a continuous battle against all of the amazing podcasts I have lined up in the queue and yet can't seem to find time to listen to. I can only run so many errands in the car or take so many walks before my wife starts to wonder whether I am leading a secret double life (I am not). Still, you'll find plenty of fodder for your own podcast battles with these three excellent sources.

- *Teaching in Higher Ed.* Bonni Stachowiak has been hosting thought leaders, authors, and innovative faculty members on her podcast for many years now; at the time of this writing; she had aired more than 350 episodes in her weekly show. I am always assured of learning something new from one of Bonni's guests, a highly diverse group of writers and educators.
- *Tea for Teaching.* I am a passionate devotee of tea in all of its many forms, so I have a soft spot for this podcast, which begins with a discussion of what tea the hosts (and guests) are drinking. The hosts are John Kane and Rebecca Mushtare, who run the Center for Excellence in Learning and Teaching at SUNY Oswego. Show times for both Teaching in Higher Ed and Tea for Teaching run in the 30–40 minute length, perfect for learning while you exercise.

- *Leading Lines.* The newest entry in this list, the Leading Lines podcast is focused on educational technology and higher education. Your host is Derek Bruff, the director of the Vanderbilt University Center for Teaching, and the author of two excellent books on teaching and technology. As with the two podcasts above, most episodes feature interviews with authors of recently published books, thought leaders in education, and creators of innovative approaches to teaching and technology.

OneHE

One of the bright spots for me in the accursed year of 2020 occurred when I was contacted by an educational start-up from the United Kingdom that was intending to build a complete resource and community site for higher education teachers based on the idea of small teaching. Their goal was to establish a place on the web which would provide not only research and resources for faculty, but also short online courses and the opportunity for faculty to engage in conversation and share with one another their problems, questions, and ideas. In all of these areas they keep their focus trained on the practical questions that I have tried to keep in front of you throughout this book: What am I doing in the classroom tomorrow? What small change could I implement to my teaching this week that would benefit my students? What design tweak could I make to the course I am teaching next semester that would re-energize both me and my students?

OneHE has done an excellent job of tapping experts from various areas of teaching and learning in higher education around the globe. A diverse range of contributors from many different disciplines is responsible for adding resources and curating the site. OneHE has been especially strong in providing resources on community building and the promotion of equity and inclusion in higher education, drawing in part on the expertise of Maha Bali from the American University of Cairo. But as the list of contributors and curators continues to expand, the scope of the site has filled out to many other areas of teaching and learning in higher education.

Both individuals and institutions can subscribe to OneHE, and I hope it will become one of the primary sources online for the ongoing development of small teaching strategies, as well as a site for like-minded enthusiasts of small teaching to form community and share ideas with one another.

SMALL TEACHING QUICK TIPS: LEARNING

My experience speaking with faculty audiences for the past dozen years has been that most of us like our work, believe in what we do, and want to improve. As in every field, though, the sheer number of resources available to us can be overwhelming. Don't imagine you need to master this body of research; just aim to keep yourself thinking.

- Commit to reading one or two new books on teaching and learning every year.
- Add one teaching-related podcast to your regular roster.
- Sign up for the regular updates from Retrieval Practice, the Learning Scientists, or OneHE. All of them send out e-mails with new updates, but none of them at an overwhelming pace; you will not find yourself inundated with new e-mails even if you subscribe to all three.
- Attend a conference on teaching and learning in higher education to expand your vision even further. Most disciplines have dedicated teaching conferences in their fields; if your discipline does not, try one of the major general conferences such as the Lilly Conferences on College and University Teaching.

- Most easily and probably most importantly, start attending events on your campus sponsored by your local faculty development center (which might go under the name of Center for Teaching Excellence, or Center for Teaching and Learning, or some other variation). You'll find both expert help and like-minded colleagues there.

CONCLUSION

Over the past six years of promoting the gospel of small teaching, I have encountered plenty of faculty members who object to the premise of this book. Small teaching, they charge, isn't enough right now. With all of the challenges facing higher education, and all of the problems we have in our societies, we need bigger change. We need revolution. I hope they are surprised to hear me respond that I agree—I am all in favor of faculty members pushing the boundaries of higher education pedagogy, experimenting with radical new approaches, and questioning traditional structures of the academy. Ken Bain, the teacher who inspired me to start researching and writing about education, has been one of these advocates for fundamental change. His most recent book, *Super Courses: The Future of Teaching and Learning*, consists of profiles of faculty members who are creating highly innovative courses that blaze new pedagogical trails. He praises these teachers for the "profound revolution" they are fomenting, the "dramatic changes" that their work can inspire, the "new breed" of courses they are developing (Bain 2021). This language of deep change is palpable throughout the book, and I find his profiles of these transformational courses and faculty members deeply inspiring. Some of the resources I have recommended above will point you toward big-teaching pathways like the one Ken Bain invites you to walk in his important works.

By no means should you take the arguments in this book, then, as advocating for the status quo. Small teaching changes can serve as a way to keep you and your students engaged within traditional courses and structures—but they can also serve as the first steps on a journey toward more revolutionary changes. For a few years I experimented with having students in my composition courses write essays to different hypothetical audiences—a small teaching strategy I recommended in Chapter Six—explaining to them that attention to audience was a fundamental feature of good writing. But one year I realized that I could best drive home this lesson by having them write to an actual, public audience. This realization was precipitated by an event in another part of my life. For many years I have served on the advisory board of a local homeless shelter, and that year our website got hacked and needed to be completely rebuilt. As I was preparing my composition course that summer, I decided that I would change my composition course assignments from hypothetical audiences to real ones. I had my students take a field trip to the homeless shelter, meet the staff and guests, interview and write profiles of them, conduct research on homelessness and poverty, and produce materials for the website. Just like that, I was doing community service learning, an approach that has totally reenergized my teaching. Community service learning is big teaching on a significant order: it requires working with a partner in the local community, planning field trips, devising completely new and different kinds of assessments, and letting go of a certain amount of control of your course. It's both profoundly satisfying and profoundly exhausting.

Small teaching led me there—and it can ultimately lead you to such places as well. The small changes you make to your teaching as a result of reading this book could translate into a regular habit of making small changes, or they may yet seed the ground for greater transformations. You might take up community service learning (Jacoby and Howard 2014), consider alternative approaches to grading (Blum 2020), or use game-based strategies like Reacting the Past (Carnes 2014). Or perhaps you will be like me, using big teaching strategies in some of your courses and more conventional small teaching strategies in others. In any given semester my composition students might be working together on a community service project, and at the same time I am teaching my British literature survey course in a much more conventional manner, sitting in a classroom and engaging in discussions about the meaning of nineteenth-century British poetry. I believe in the value of both of these approaches.

But whether you keep your teaching small and conventional or expand it into radical new territories, rest assured that there are resources out there to guide you in your journey. If you are ready to keep learning, you'll find plenty of excellent teachers out there to help you along the way.

Conclusion: Beginning

The ultimate aim of this book has been to convince you that you can create powerful learning for your students through the small, everyday decisions you make in designing your courses, engaging in classroom practice, communicating with your students, and addressing any challenges that arise. Even if you find that none of the specific strategies mentioned in this book work for you, I still hope that you will have been convinced that small steps can make a big difference. If you are an instructor, take the models and principles that I have described in this book and adapt them into your courses; if they don't fit, use them instead as inspiration to create your own small teaching strategies. Make an effort to measure the effects of changes that you implement so you can understand how to improve them or when to abandon them if they are not working. You can find plenty of excellent means of measuring the learning of your students, and the effectiveness of specific teaching techniques, in Angelo and Cross's now classic (and still excellent) *Classroom Assessment Techniques* (Angelo and Cross 1993). You can also use quick midterm surveys and end-of-course evaluations for measurement purposes. Linda Nilson's *Teaching at Its Best* contains an excellent overview chapter on documenting and measuring the effectiveness of your teaching with such methods (Nilson 2010).

The best aid, though, to help you initiate and gauge the success of new teaching techniques may be right on your campus, in the form of your center for teaching excellence, center for teaching and learning, or whatever other name it might be called. There you are likely to find someone who will be thrilled to hear that you are trying new strategies to boost student learning in your courses, who has plenty of experience in implementing and measuring teaching effectiveness, and who will be very glad to assist you at both ends of the process. If you are one of those faculty development professionals, I hope you can use the small teaching framework as a way to gather faculty together and work with them to brainstorm new ways to create powerful learning for students on your campus. What are the common challenges that faculty on your campus are facing right now? Can small thinking, like small teaching, lead to new solutions to those problems?

For now, you probably have class tomorrow morning, or at least within the next week. Think about the first five minutes of that next class period. You could give students a little retrieval practice by spending those opening minutes asking them to answer some questions, either orally or in writing, about the material you covered in the last class or about the reading they completed for homework. You could prepare them for the day's content by asking them to make a prediction about a problem you will be presenting in your opening mini-lecture. You could throw up a fascinating image and ask them to wonder about it. Perhaps you will even get to class five minutes early and make an effort to engage in some informal discussion with a student who has not spoken in class this semester and who just might benefit from some quick social interaction with her instructor.

You also have class next semester. How can you use the theory of prediction to create an opening-day activity that will activate the prior knowledge of your students and prepare them for learning? How can you ensure that students will continually cycle back to the material they have already learned, to take advantage of the learning power of.spacing and interleaving? Where might a day spent on the Minute Thesis game pack the most learning punch for your students? What about your written communications with them? Can you revise the language of your syllabus to normalize help-seeking behaviors? Will you modify the language you use when you give feedback to your students to ensure that it promotes a sense of belonging? And how can you let students know about the ways practitioners in your field are making the world a better place—and the ways they might do so someday as well?

Finally, you have a teaching career ahead of you, however long or short that might be at this point in your life. You could continue to explore and experiment with small teaching strategies for another 20 or 30 years and probably still not exhaust the possibilities. Perhaps over time you will recognize that students in your introductory and survey courses need more retrieval practice and motivational talk, whereas students in your upper-level seminars really need to do more connecting and explaining. Perhaps you were intrigued by the description of learning as connection-making, and now you wish to dig into some of the books that I have referenced and recommended in these pages. Or maybe you will push yourself further and explore alternative pedagogies like community service learning or ungrading. If you have been inspired even more deeply, perhaps you will gather a group of colleagues together to share your best ideas for small teaching and learn from one another in addition to learning from the literature on teaching and learning in higher education. The prospects can be as wide or narrow as you wish.

Most important, you have class tomorrow morning.

How will you begin?

Works Cited

Agarwal, P. (2019). What is retrieval practice? *Retrieval Practice.* https://www.retrievalpractice.org/why-it-works.

Agarwal, P., & Bain, P. (2019). *Powerful teaching: Unleash the science of learning.* San Francisco: Jossey-Bass.

Ambrose, S., Bridges, M., DiPietro, M., Lovett, M., & Norman, M. (2010). *How learning works: Seven research-based principles for smart teaching.* San Francisco, CA: Jossey-Bass.

Ambrose, S. A., & Lovett, M. C. (2014). Prior knowledge is more than content: Skills and beliefs also impact learning. In V. A. Benassi, C. E. Overson, & C. M. Hakala (Eds.), *Applying science of learning in education: Infusing psychological science into the curriculum* (pp. 7–19). Retrieved from http://www.teachpsych.org/Resources/Documents/ebooks/asle2014.pdf.

Angelo, T. A., & Cross, K. P. (1993). *Classroom assessment techniques: A handbook for college teachers.* San Francisco, CA: Jossey-Bass.

Bain, K. (2004). *What the best college teachers do.* Cambridge, MA: Harvard University Press.

Bain, K. (2021). *Super courses: The future of teaching and learning.* Princeton, NJ: Princeton UP.

Banning, M. (2004). The think aloud approach as an educational tool to develop and assess clinical reasoning in undergraduate students. *Nurse Education Today,* **28**, 8–14.

Blazer, A. (2014). Student summaries of class sessions. *Teaching Theology and Religion,* **17**(4), 344.

Bloom, K. C., & Shuell, T. J. (1981). Effects of massed and distributed practice on the learning and retention of second-language vocabulary. *Journal of Educational Research,* **74**(4), 245–248.

Blum, S., ed. (2020). *Ungrading: Why grading students undermines learning (and what to do instead)*. Morgantown, WV: West Virginia UP.

Brod, G. (2021, March 25). Predicting as a learning strategy. *Psychonomic Bulletin and Review*, https://link.springer.com/article/10.3758/s13423-021-01904-1.

Brown, P. C., Roediger, H. L., & McDaniel, M. A. (2014). *Make it stick: The science of successful learning*. Cambridge, MA: Harvard University Press.

Bruff, D. (2009). *Teaching with classroom response systems: Creative active learning environments*. San Francisco, CA: Jossey-Bass.

Canning, E., Muenks, K., Green, D., & Murphy, M. (2019, February 15). STEM faculty who believe ability is fixed have larger racial achievement gaps and inspire less student motivation in their classes. *Science Advances* 5(2). Retrieved from https://advances.sciencemag.org/content/5/2/eaau4734.

Carey, B. (2014a). *How we learn: The surprising truth about when, where, and why it happens*. New York, NY: Random House.

Carey, B. (2014b, September 4). Why flunking exams is actually a good thing. *New York Times*. http://www.nytimes.com/2014/09/07/magazine/why-flunking-exams-is-actually-a-good-thing.html.

Carnes, M. (2014). *Minds on fire: How role-immersion games transform college*. Cambridge, MA: Harvard University Press.

Carpenter, S. K., & Mueller, F. E. (2013). The effects of interleaving versus blocking on foreign language pronunciation learning. *Memory and Cognition*, **41**(5), 671–682.

Cavanagh, Sarah. (2016). *The spark of learning: Energizing the college classroom with the science of emotion*. Morgantown, WV: West Virginia University Press.

Center for First-Generation Student Success. (2020). National data fact sheets. https://firstgen.naspa.org/research-and-policy/national-data-fact-sheets-on-first-generation-college-students/national-data-fact-sheets.

Chambliss, D. F., & Takacs, C. J. (2014). *How college works*. Cambridge, MA: Harvard University Press.

Chi, M. T. H., Bassok, M., Lewis, M. W., Reimann, P., & Glaser, R. (1989). Self-explanations: How students study and use examples in learning to solve problems. *Cognitive Science*, **13**, 145–182.

Chi, M. T. H., DeLeeuw, N., Chiu, M.-H., & LaVancher, C. (1994). Eliciting self-explanations improves understanding. *Cognitive Science*, **18**, 439–477.

Chiu, J., & Chi, M. T. H. (2014). Supporting self-explanation in the classroom. In V. A. Benassi, C. E. Overson, & C. M. Hakala (Eds.), *Applying science of learning in education: Infusing psychological science into the curriculum.* (pp. 91–103). Retrieved from http://www.teachpsych.org/Resources/Documents/ebooks/asle2014.pdf.

Coleman, E. B., Brown, A. L., & Rivkin, I. D. (1997). The effect of instructional explanations on learning from scientific texts. *Journal of the Learning Sciences, 6*(4), 347–365.

Cornelius, T. L., & Owen-DeSchryver, J. (2008). Differential effects of full and partial notes on learning outcomes and attendance. *Teaching of Psychology*, **35**, 6–12.

Darby, F. with Lang, J. (2019). *Small teaching online: Applying learning science in online classes.* San Francisco: Jossey-Bass.

DeAngelis, T. (2019).College students mental health is a higher priority. *Monitor on Psychology* **50**(11), 80.

Deci, E.L. with Flaste, R. (1996). *Why We Do What We Do: Understanding Self-Motivation.* New York: Penguin.

Dehaene, S. (2020). *How we learn: Why brains learn better than any machine . . . for now.* New York: Viking.

Denworth, L. (2019, August 12). Debate arises over teaching "growth mindsets" to motivate students. *Scientific American.* https://www.scientificamerican.com/article/debate-arises-over-teaching-growth-mindsets-to-motivate-students/.

Dunlovsky, J. (2013). Strengthening the student toolbox: study strategies to boost learning. *American Educator, 37*(3), 12–21.

Dweck, C. (2008). *Mindset: The new psychology of success.* New York, NY: Ballantine.

Emdin, C. (2016). *For white folks who teach in the hood . . . and the rest of y'all too*. Boston: Beacon.

Eyler, J. (2018). *How humans learn: The science and stories behind effective college teaching*. Morgantown, WV: West Virginia University Press.

Fiorella, L., & Mayer, R. (2013). The relative benefits of learning by teaching and teaching expectancy. *Contemporary Educational Psychology* 38, 281–288.

Fishman, S.M., & Wahesh, E. (2020). The F3: faculty feedback forms for students. *College Teaching*. https://www.tandfonline.com/doi/full/10.1080/87567555.2020.1814685.

Flipped classroom model shows proven progress in addressing broken educational experience in U.S. (2013, November 9). Sonic Foundry. http://www.sonicfoundry.com/press-release/flipped-classroom-model-shows-proven-progress-addressing-broken-educational-experience.

Fogg, BJ. (2020). *Tiny habits: The small changes that change everything*. Boston: Houghton Mifflin Harcourt.

Gharravi, A.M. (2018). Impact of instructor-provided notes on the learning and exam performance of medical students in an organ system-based medical curriculum. *Advanced Medical Education Practice* 9, 665–672.

Goldrick-Rab, S. (2017, August 7). Basic needs security and the syllabus. *Medium*. https://saragoldrickrab.medium.com/basic-needs-security-and-the-syllabus-d24cc7afe8c9.

Gooblar, D. (2019). *The missing course: Everything they never taught you about college teaching*. Cambridge: Harvard UP.

Gregory, S. (2014a, October 29). Dynasty! The San Francisco Giants win it all. *Time*.

Gregory, S. (2014b, October 15). The Kansas City Royals are the future of baseball. *Time*.

Gurung, R., & Galardi, N. (2021, February 11). Syllabus tone, more than mental health statements, influence intentions to seek help. *Teaching of Psychology*.

Howard, J. (2015). *Discussion in the college classroom: Getting your students engaged and participating in person and online.* San Francisco, CA: Jossey-Bass.

Hoyle, J. (2012, June 3). How to make an A. E-mail to author.

Jacoby, B., & Howard, J. (2014). *Service-learning essentials: Questions, answers, and lessons learned.* San Francisco, CA: Jossey-Bass.

James, W. (1900). *Talks to teachers and students.* New York: Henry Holt and Co.

Keaney, K. (2018). Waiting for your students. D'Amour Center for Teaching Excellence, Assumption University. Retrieved from http://www1.assumption.edu/cte/damour-student-fellows/2018-2019-student-fellow-essays/kelliann-keaney-waiting-for-your-students/.

Khanna, M. M., Badura Brack, A. S., & Finken, L. L. (2013). Short- and long-term effects of cumulative finals on student learning. *Teaching of Psychology,* **40**(3), 175–182.

Kobayashi, K. (2019). Learning by preparing-to-teach and teaching: a meta-analysis. *Japanese Psychological Research* 61(3), 192–203.

Kornell, N., Jenson Hayes, M., & Bjork, R. A. (2009). Unsuccessful retrieval attempts enhance subsequent learning. *Journal of Experimental Psychology: Learning, Memory, and Cognition,* **35**(4), 989–998.

Kray, L. J., & Haselhuhn, M. P. (2007). Implicit negotiation beliefs and performance: Experimental and longitudinal evidence. *Journal of Personality and Social Psychology,* **93**(1), 49–64.

Lahey, J. (2015). *The gift of failure: How the best parents learn to let go so their children can succeed.* New York: Harper.

Lang, J. (2013). *Cheating lessons: Learning from academic dishonesty.* Cambridge, MA: Harvard University Press.

Lang, J. (2015, March 30). The three essential functions of your syllabus, part 2. *Chronicle of Higher Education.* Retrieved from https://www.chronicle.com/article/the-3-essential-functions-of-your-syllabus-part-2/.

Lang, J. (2020). *Distracted: Why students can't focus and what you can do about it.* New York: Basic Books.

Langer, E. J. (1997). *The power of mindful learning*. Cambridge, MA: DaCapo.

Leslie, I. (2015). *Curious: The Desire to Know and Why Your Future Depends On it*. New York: Basic Books.

Lozano, G. (2020, July 9). Simply scrapping the SAT won't make colleges more diverse. *The Conversation*. https://theconversation.com/simply-scrapping-the-sat-wont-make-colleges-more-diverse-140042.

McGuire, S. (2015). *Teach students how to learn: Strategies you can incorporate into any course to improve student metacognition, study skills, and motivation*. Sterling, VA: Stylus.

Miller, M. (2011). What college teachers should know about memory: A perspective from cognitive psychology. *College Teaching, 59*, 117–122.

Miller, M. (2014). *Minds online: Teaching effectively with technology*. Cambridge, MA: Harvard University Press.

Morris, P., Gruneberg, M., Sykes, R., & Merrick, A. (1981). Football knowledge and the acquisition of new results. *British Journal of Psychology, 72*(4), 479–483.

Mueller, C. M., & Dweck, C. S. (1998). Praise for intelligence can undermine children's motivation and performance. *Journal of Personality and Social Psychology, 75*(1), 33–52.

Nadworny, E. (2018). "'Going to office hours is terrifying' and other tales of rural students in college." *NPR Morning Edition 12 Decmeber* 2018. https://www.npr.org/2018/12/12/668530699/-going-to-office-hours-is-terrifying-and-other-hurdles-for-rural-students-in-col.

Nelson, L. (2010). *Teaching at its best: A research-based resource for college instructors*. (5th ed.). San Francisco: Jossey-Bass.

Oakley, B., Rogowsky, B., & Sejnowski, T. (2021). *Uncommon sense teaching: Practical insights in brain science to help students learn*. New York: TarcherPerigee.

Ogan, A., Aleven, V., & Jones, C. (2009). Advancing development of intercultural competence through supporting predictions in narrative video. *International Journal of Artificial Intelligence in Education, 19*(3), 267–288.

Orwell, G. (1986). *A clergyman's daughter*. London, UK: Penguin Books.

Orwell, G. (1968). My country right or left: 1940–1943. In S. Orwell & I. Angus (Eds.), *The collected essays, journalism, and letters of George Orwell*. New York: Harcourt, Brace, and World, Inc.

Paunesku, D., Walton, G. M., Romero, C., Smith, E. N., Yeager, D. S., & Dweck, C. S. (2015, April 10). Mind-set interventions are a scalable treatment for academic underachievement. *Psychological Science, April* 10, 1–10.

Pyc, M. A., Agarwal, P. K., & Roediger III, H. L. (2014). Test-enhanced learning. In V. A. Benassi, C. E. Overson, & C. M. Hakala (Eds.), *Applying science of learning in education: Infusing psychological science into the curriculum*. American Psychological Association Society for the *Teaching of Psychology*. Retrieved from http://www.teachpsych.org/Resources/Documents/ebooks/asle2014.pdf.

Roediger III, H. L., & Butler, A. C. (2007). Testing improves long-term retention in a simulated classroom setting. *European Journal of Cognitive Psychology*, **19**, 514–527.

Rogerson, B. (2003). Effectiveness of a daily class progress assessment technique in introductory chemistry. *Journal of Chemical Education*, **80**(2), 160–164.

Rohrer, D., & Taylor, K. (2007). The shuffling of mathematics problems improves learning. *Instructional Science*, **35**(6), 481–498.

Sathy, V. & Hogan, K. (2019, July 22). How to make your teaching more inclusive. *Chronicle of Higher Education*. Retrieved from https://www.chronicle.com/article/how-to-make-your-teaching-more-inclusive/.

Schell, J. (2012, March 15). Peer instruction 101: What is peer instruction? *Turn to Your Neighbor: The Official Peer Instruction Blog*. http://blog.peerinstruction.net/2012/03/15/peer-instruction-101-what-is-peer-instruction/.

Talbert, R. (2014, April 28). Flipped learning skepticism: Is flipped learning just self-teaching? *Chronicle of Higher Education*. Retrieved from http://chronicle.com/blognetwork/castingoutnines/2014/04/28/flipped-learning-skepticism-is-flipped-learning-just-self-teaching/.

U.S. Department of Education, National Center for Education Statistics. (2019). *Digest of Education Statistics, 2018.* https://nces.ed.gov/programs/digest/d18/ch_3.asp.

Weimer, M. (2015, March 18). Using cumulative exams to help students revisit, review, and retain course content. *Faculty Focus.* Retrieved from http://www.facultyfocus.com/articles/teaching-professor-blog/using-cumulative-exams-help-students-revisit-review-retain-course-content/.

Weinstein, Y. and Sumeracki, M., with Caviglioli, O. (2019). *Understanding how we learn: A visual guide.* London and New York: Routledge.

Willingham, D. (2009). *Why don't students like school? A cognitive scientist answers questions about how the mind works and what it means for the classroom.* San Francisco: Jossey-Bass.

Wrzesniewsk, A., Schwartz, B., Cong, X., Kane, M., Omar, A., & Kolditz, T. (2014). Multiple types of motives don't multiply the motivation of West Point cadets. *Proceedings of the National Academy of Sciences of the United States of America,* **111**(30), 10990–10995.

Yeager, D., Henderson, M., Paunesku, D., Walton, G., D'Mello, S., Spitzer, B., & Duckworth, A. (2014). Boring but important: a self-transcendent purpose for learning fosters academic self-regulation. *Journal of Personality and Social Psychology* **107**(4), 559–580.

Yeager, D. et al. (2019). A national experiment reveals where a growth mindset improves achievement. *Nature* 573, 364-369. Retrieved from https://www.nature.com/articles/s41586-019-1466-y.

Zull, J. (2002). *The art of changing the brain: Enriching the practice of teaching by exploring the biology of learning.* Sterling, VA: Stylus.

Index